THE INTERNATIONAL GRANDMOTHERS' COOKBOOK

Favorite recipes
of grandmothers from
around the world

By Eileen Weppner

Blue
Mountain
Arts, inc.

Boulder, Colorado

Library of Congress Catalog Number: 73-86814
ISBN Number: 0-88396-003-6

Manufactured in the United States of America

Acknowledgements: All photographs by
Jerry Stowall except the photographs
in chapter on Rae Keller, which are by
Stephen Schutz. Edited and created by
Susan Polis Schutz. Thanks to the
grandmothers, without whose cooperation
this book would not exist.

All comments and remarks on recipes
should be sent to Blue Mountain Arts, Inc.

BLUE MOUNTAIN ARTS, INC.
P.O. Box 4549
Boulder, Colorado 80302

First Printing, January, 1974
Second Printing, April, 1974

INTRODUCTION

Everyone knows how warm and charming grandmothers from the "old country" are. This is reflected in their speech, dress, and of course their cooking.

The International Grandmothers' Cookbook, written by Eileen Weppner, gives us grandmothers' recipes which have been passed down from generation to generation. Though the recipes originate in different countries, they all emphasize natural fresh ingredients. In addition to the recipes, Eileen recreates the cultural background of the grandmothers with brief biographical sketches.

Many of us have forgotten the ways of our grandmothers. We have assimilated into communities so well that there is no evidence of who we are or where we come from.

We hope that in addition to learning new, but old, delicious ways of cooking from this book, you will also be inspired to absorb some of the culture of our ancestors.

Susan Polis Schutz

CONTENTS

JAPANESE

Miyeko Ogata dips a shrimp in the *tempura* batter, holding it securely between two cooking chopsticks, then releases it into the large, *wok*-like pan of hot oil, where pieces of green pepper and green beans are already frying. "You don't put too many in at once," she warns, "and you don't let any fragments stay in the oil. I use salad oil, and save it to use over. It's better to use half used oil and half fresh, because all brand new oil does not give the golden color. And you don't let the tail of the shrimp get in the batter, or you lose the pretty pink color. Another secret is to use ice water in the egg batter; when it's colder, it's better."

Flat aluminum *sukiyaki* platters sit on the kitchen table, holding gracefully arranged, bite-size pieces of thin-sliced beef, bamboo shoots, green pepper and scallion strips, and one-inch squares of *tofu*, a bland soybean curd of custard consistency. Thin cucumber slices marinated in vinegar are ready, the *suimono*, or soup, is hot, and the automatic electric rice cooker has steamed a generous amount of rice. In an unflustered countdown, Miyeko keeps the shrimp and vegetables going through the *tempura* process and sets the *sukiyaki* platters on the electric burners, which they fit exactly. "In wintertime it's nice to cook the *sukiyaki* on the table," Miyeko remarks. "Then you can taste it as it cooks."

Soon everything is on the table, as appealing to the eye as to the taste buds. The cucumber slices are served in square blue-and-white porcelain bowls whose sides are topped by a triangular edging. The rice is served plain in a separate bowl, and adding to the array of dishes at each place are a soup bowl, a plate of *tempura*, and a small bowl of sauce to dip the *tempura* in. A bottle of *shoyu* is often placed on a Japanese table, but never salt or pepper. Although there is egg *suimono*, only chopsticks are needed; they are used for picking up pieces of cooked egg, and the soup itself is simply drunk from the bowl.

However, dessert, a simple sherbet, does require a spoon. "Japanese don't eat much of a dessert," says Miyeko. "After dinner they like to eat fruits, especially mandarin oranges, sherbet or ice cream, or Japanese jellies called *kanten.* These are flavored and similar to Jell-O, but instead of gelatin, they are made with *kanten* sticks, which are made out of seaweed. And that is *gen mai* tea. My daughter calls it 'popcorn' tea, from the special taste of the toasted rice or wheat in it." This is one of Japan's many green teas, and no Japanese would think of adding sugar, much less milk. It is served in small cups without handles which rest on wooden coasters of plum blossom shape.

Sake, Japanese rice wine, is often served with dinner in special thimble-size cups called *sakazuki.* Brewed by fermenting rice and then distilling it, *sake* has an alcohol content of 15 to 20 percent. It may be drunk cold, but most Japanese prefer it warmed, to bring out its delicate aromas and flavors. They fill beautiful small porcelain bottles called *tokkuri* with *sake,* and heat them in hot water before bringing them to the table, where a cup-exchanging ritual is often followed.

"For New Year's Day," says Miyeko, "it is traditional to have *tai,* a fish which looks like a large red snapper. They cook the head and tail, because it would be bad luck to chop them off, and they broil it with the tail curved up so it looks pretty, instead of flat down. With Japanese food, everything is artistic; everything is beautifully arranged. They care more about what it looks like than the taste, I sometimes think! New Year's is the biggest holiday all year, and the first day of the year is supposed to count for good luck. My parents used to say if you cry on it, you will be crying all year."

Mochi, rice cakes, are also eaten on New Year's, by themselves, or placed in a clear soup called *ozoni.* They symbolize wealth, since *mochi* also means "to have." The cakes are formed from a sticky dough obtained by pounding hot steamed rice in wooden tubs. Of course, *mochi* may also be bought frozen, or made from dry *mochi-gome* mix which comes in boxes. This New Year's emphasis on rice is only fitting, since rice provides half the calories in the Japanese diet. *Gohan,* the Japanese word for rice, also means food in general. As Miyeko observes, "Rice is our bread."

Soybeans, imported from the United States, are another mainstay of Japanese cooking. They are made into *shoyu,* or Japanese soy sauce; the fermented soybean paste called *miso*; and *tofu.* All three are sold in oriental or specialty food stores in larger American cities, and even in many supermarkets. The easiest to find is *shoyu,* usually under the brand name of Kikkoman, Japan's largest *shoyu* exporter. Because Chinese soy sauce is produced by a fast hydrochlorination process and contains additives, whereas *shoyu* is fermented naturally and then aged, the two are completely different in taste.

Miso, like *shoyu*, flavors a variety of dishes; it may be purchased in one-pound-size plastic bags. A nutritious and flavorful concentrate of amino acids, natural sugars, oils, vitamins, and trace minerals, it is the essential ingredient in the soup called *miso-shiru.* *Tofu,* with its pleasant but mild flavor, harmonizes with any and every dish. It is mixed with scrambled eggs or sesame seeds, boiled, broiled, and even deep-fat-fried. *Tofu* cubes are very good eaten cold, expecially when dipped in a sauce of grated fresh ginger and *shoyu.* *Tofu* may be bought fresh, in cans, or in instant powdered form. Soybean products are particularly important in regions of Japan where fish is scarce, and among vegetarians, since soybeans contain about three times as much protein as dry beans or peas, very little sugar, and no starch. They also provide essential amino acids, calcium, and B vitamins.

Seaweed, a rich source of minerals and vitamins, provides about ten percent of the food eaten by Japanese. The variety called laver is pressed into thin sheets and sun-dried, and the *nori* thus produced is wrapped around rice and other foods, or crumbled up and sprinkled over them. *Kombu* is a kind of kelp, used along with *katsuobushi* (dried bonito flakes) and *Ajinomoto* (monosodium glutamate) to make *dashi*, the basic Japanese soup stock. These seaweeds are stocked in oriental food stores, as are "teabags" of dry *dashi* mix, and bags of dried *shitake*, the mushroom most used in Japanese cooking. Ginger root, often available in supermarkets, is also used in many Japanese recipes. Miyeko says, "We used to have a little pot just for ginger, and preserve it buried in the ground.

"We used to have a woodburning stove," she recalls. "They still use them in the country, but those days are gone. City people use gas and electric. I think rice cooked on the old-fashioned stove is better!" Although Miyeko was born in the United States, her parents came from Wakayama, near Osaka, and she returned to Japan for about ten years to attend high school and finishing school. Now a widow, she still runs the very successful Mikado Gift Shop in Boulder, Colorado, which she and her husband started 18 years ago.

"At finishing school we studied the tea ceremony, flower arrangements, and a musical instrument," Miyeko says. "It takes several years to learn to do the tea ceremony, and the ceremony might take two or three hours."

Kaiseki ryori, "tea ceremony cooking," is the highest expression of the Japanese belief that food should please the eye and the mind, as well as the palate. The foods chosen, and their colors and shapes, subtly echo the season, the surroundings, the special occasion, and even the time of day — the large mushrooms called *matsutake* in October, circular shapes for an *otsukimi,* a moon viewing. But ostentation is never allowed; the foods chosen are simple, inexpensive, and, if possible, obtained nearby.

Although the few guests at a tea ceremony talk quietly to each other, the conversation is as stylized and graceful as the choreographed motions of the host or hostess. Articles used in the ceremony, often of considerable value and beauty, are admired and commented upon according to an elaborate etiquette, and every word and action reflects the Zen ideal of simplicity and serenity.

"You inspect the charcoal in the brazier, and the teakettle on top of it," says Miyeko. "*Chashaku* is the name of the bamboo spoon you use to scoop tea into the bowl. It's very finely powdered green tea called *matcha*; the Japanese have had instant tea for hundreds of years! The long-handled bamboo dipper is a *hishaku*. With it you scoop the hot water and put it in the *chawan*, tea bowl. Finally, the little bamboo whisk called a *chasen* is used to whip up the hot tea in the bowl, and you present it to the guest. It is a very deep ceremony, developed by Zen Buddhist monks in the fifteenth century. It's too slow for here, but in Japan they take time with everything. They don't just drink tea; they taste it. They meditate, and have a different kind of quiet."

"In Japan they don't just drink tea, they taste it"

EGG FLOWER *SUIMONO* (CLEAR SOUP)

SOUP
6 cups chicken or pork stock (boil chicken skins and bones, or
   1/2 cup cut-up pork, in water 30 minutes and then strain; or
   use "tea bags" or pellets of *Dashi-no-Moto* soup stock sold
   in oriental or specialty stores)
1 teaspoon salt
3/4 cup cooked, coarsely
   chopped pork or chicken breast
1/2 cup onion, minced
1/2 cup water chestnuts, sliced
   (optional)
1/2 cup mushrooms, sliced
   (optional)
1/4 teaspoon monosodium glutamate*
1/2 cup bamboo sprouts, sliced
   (optional)
a few drops of *shoyu* for color

EGG FLOWER BATTER
1 teaspoon cornstarch   1 tablespoon cold water
2 eggs

Combine soup ingredients and bring to a boil. Simmer 30
minutes. Add *shoyu* to obtain desired color. Put egg flower batter
ingredients in separate bowl and mix well. Gradually trickle batter
into the simmering soup; a slotted spoon makes this easier. The
egg will float in thin threads on the soup. Serves 6 to 8.

SUKIYAKI (SIMMERED BEEF AND VEGETABLES)

TO BE FRIED
1/2 pound sirloin tip beef,   4 green onions, cut into
   sliced very thin (let stiffen 1/2   1 1/2-inch pieces
   hour in freezer before slicing)   1 cake *tofu*, cut into
enough cubed beef suet to   1-inch cubes
   grease fry pan

---

*Monosodium glutamate enhances flavor, but it should not be
used in excess.

1 small can sliced bamboo
shoots (optional)
1 large onion, sliced thin
2 stalks celery, in 1/4-inch
diagonal slices

1/2 pound white mushrooms, in
1/4-inch slices

SAUCE
3/4 cup meat broth
1 tablespoon sugar

1/4 cup *shoyu*

ANOTHER SAUCE
equal amounts of *shoyu* and *sake* (or pale dry sherry), with a
little sugar added, to taste

Mix sauce ingredients, heat, and keep in bowl at table. Arrange
vegetables and meat in rows on large platter. Put electric fry pan
on medium heat on or near dining table. Rub suet around the
fry pan and remove. Stir half the beef around pan until no longer
pink, and push to the side. Put half the mushrooms in one part of
fry pan and half the celery and onions in another part. Add about
half the cooking sauce and simmer about 15 minutes, stirring
occasionally, and lowering heat as needed. About 5 minutes before
these ingredients are done, add remaining mushrooms,
tofu cubes, rest of cooking sauce, and bamboo shoots (if desired).
Turn heat to low and serve at once. Serves 3 to 4.

TEMPURA (DEEP-FRIED SEAFOOD AND VEGETABLES)

BATTER*
2 eggs
1 cup unsifted flour

1 cup ice-cold water
1/2 teaspoon salt

SAUCE (mix ingredients thoroughly)
3 cups fish stock or other *dashi*
1/2 teaspoon monosodium glutamate
4 tablespoons *shoyu*
4 tablespoons *mirin* (or pale
dry sherry)

FOR FRYING
sesame oil, salad oil, or a combination of the two

SEAFOODS AND VEGETABLES (select those you prefer ; all except green beans are uncooked)

boneless pieces of fish (white-flesh) small enough to eat in 1 or 2 bites

crab chunks

drained oysters, clams, and scallops, cut in half

shrimp, peeled and deveined, but with tails left on

1/2-inch diagonal slices of asparagus

1/4-inch slices of eggplant

green beans, cooked 5 minutes, drained, dried, and cut into 2-inch lengths

sweet potato, peeled and sliced thin

mushrooms, cut in half

fresh snow peas, or frozen snow peas which have been thawed

canned ginkgo nuts, drained

green peppers, sliced thin

sliced lobster tails

carrots and celery, sliced thin

When the seafood and vegetables are ready, heat 3 inches of oil to from 350 degrees to 375 degrees. If you have no deep-fat thermometer, put a drop of batter in the oil: if it sinks to the bottom and slowly rises, the oil is not hot enough; if it does not sink but stays at top, the oil is too hot; if it sinks and then rises rapidly to the surface and spins around, the oil is in the right temperature range. Combine eggs and ice-cold water and beat until fluffy. Mix salt and unsifted flour, and add to egg batter. Beat until blended, but do not overbeat. Set bowl of batter in a bowl of ice so that it will stay cold. Using chopsticks, fork, or tongs, dip seafood and vegetables (one at a time) into batter, let drip a moment, and then cook in hot oil until browned on all sides. Drain on paper towels and serve hot with individual bowls of hot sauce in which to dip the *tempura*. It is best to complete one person's serving at a time and let him start eating while you fry the next person's, but *tempura* may be kept warm in a 250-degree oven for no more than 5 minutes. Keep skimming off loose bits of *tempura* and batter to keep the oil clean.

---

* If you need more batter, make in batches this size as needed, instead of doubling this recipe. If batter is allowed to stand, results will be disappointing.

CHAWAN MUSHI (MAIN-DISH CUSTARD)

2 cups uncooked chicken, cut
into small slivers
6 eggs, well beaten (one egg
per cup of *chawan mushi*)
1/2 cup green onions, in
1/2-inch pieces (some people
prefer a little fresh spinach)
1/2 cup frozen peas, thawed
4 cups water
salt, to taste

1/2 cup canned or fresh
mushrooms
1/2 teaspoon monosodium
glutamate
6 *chawan mushi* dishes, or
custard cups

Cook chicken slices in water and monosodium glutamate until tender, about 20 minutes. Remove from heat and cool. Take out chicken and set aside. Add eggs to the liquid, mixing thoroughly. Fill 6 lidded *chawan mushi* bowls (or custard cups) with equal amounts of cooked chicken, peas, green onions, and mushrooms. Pour equal amounts of beaten egg liquid into each bowl. Set the bowls in an oriental steamer or in a pan containing 1 to 2 inches of boiling water, so that water comes about half-way up sides of bowls. If using custard cups, lay a cookie sheet or layer cake pan across their tops, or cover each with aluminum foil. Let bowls or cups steam in boiling water on top of stove until the custard is firm in the center when the cup or bowl is shaken, about 10 to 20 minutes, but do not overcook. Serve hot in same bowls or cups. Serves 6.

Other commonly used *chawan mushi* ingredients are cooked shrimp (peeled and deveined), bamboo sprouts, and canned ginkgo nuts.

PINEAPPLE KANTEN

3 sticks *kanten*
3 cups sugar
20-ounce can crushed pineapple,
well drained

4 1/2 cups water
3 teaspoons vanilla or lemon
extract

Kanten (agar-agar) is made from seaweed and contains no calories. Unlike gelatin, it congeals at room temperature. It may be bought in the form of translucent sticks at oriental stores, health food stores, and other specialty stores. To use, crumble *kanten* into small pieces and soak 30 minutes in water, which will make it swell. Squeeze all the water out of the *kanten* and put *kanten* in a saucepan. Add 4 1/2 cups water and boil until *kanten* is completely dissolved. Add the sugar and bring to a boil again. Remove from heat, and mix in pineapple and flavoring. Pour into a pan about 10 inches x 14 inches in size. Cool, and serve in slices. Serves about 6.

CHIRASHIZUSHI (VINEGARED RICE WITH SEAFOOD AND VEGETABLES)

1 package frozen green peas
   (or fresh peas)
6 large shitake (dried mushrooms)
1 stick *kamaboko* (fish cake)
4 cups water
2 tablespoons sugar
monosodium glutamate, to taste
2 medium carrots, finely slivered
6 shrimp, cooked, cut in half,
   and soaked in sugar and vinegar
1 can (8 1/2 ounces) bamboo shoots
5 beaten eggs, mixed with a little
   sugar and salt, and a dash of monosodium
   glutamate, to taste

a little fresh ginger root
3 1/2 cups uncooked rice
1/2 cup white vinegar
1 1/2 teaspoon salt

PREPARING RICE
Wash rice well several times until water is clear, and drain. Add the same water again, with salt. Let stand 15 minutes. Cover, put over medium heat 5 minutes, lower heat, and boil 15 minutes longer. Remove from heat and let stand with lid on for 10 minutes. Let rice cool in shallow container. Mix and heat vinegar, sugar, salt, and monosodium glutamate. Rapidly stir this mixture into the rice. When rice reaches room temperature, it is ready to serve.

PREPARING OTHER FOODS
Soak *shitake* 15 minutes in warm water. Remove stalks and boil in water and monosodium glutamate until tender. Add a little

sugar and boil 5 minutes. Add some *shoyu* and boil it away. Mix eggs with a little sugar, salt, and monosodium glutamate, to taste; fry very thin. Slice up this thin omelet. Chop up the fish cake. Sprinkle peas over rice, then omelet slices, then shredded ginger root. Sprinkle carrots, shrimp, bamboo shoots, and *shitake* over rice. Other vegetables and seafoods may be used, as desired. Serves 6.

SUNOMONO (VINEGARED DISHES)

SALAD

2 cucumbers	2 teaspoons salt for cucumbers
2 cups shredded carrots	1/4 teaspoon salt for carrots
small can of cocktail shrimp, sliced (optional)	

DRESSING

1/2 cup sugar	1/2 cup rice vinegar (or ordinary white vinegar)

Peel cucumbers, but leave a little skin on for green color. Cut into paper-thin slices, sprinkle with 2 teaspoons salt, and chill. Grate carrots, sprinkle with 1/4 teaspoon salt, and mix with cucumber slices. Mix in shrimp slices. Mix sugar and vinegar until sugar dissolves, and pour this mixture over salad, mixing well. Serves 4 to 5.

FOUR OTHER DRESSINGS

1. equal amounts of white vinegar and *shoyu**, or half as much *shoyu* as vinegar
2. equal amounts of vinegar, *shoyu,* and sugar
3. 1/4 cup strained *miso,* 2 tablespoons vinegar, 2 tablespoons sugar, 1/2 teaspoon monosodium glutamate
4. 1/2 cup vinegar, 1/2 cup *mirin***, 2 tablespoons sugar, 2 teaspoons *shoyu*

---

*Never substitute Chinese soy sauce for Japanese soy sauce (*shoyu*). They are completely different.
**Mirin* is a sweet rice wine. Pale dry sherry may be substituted for it.

JEWISH

The delicious smell of roasting chicken fills Rae Keller's small Brooklyn kitchen as she stands at the stove, dish towel on her wrist ready for action. ''Jewish cooking is good health cooking,'' she says, peeking into pots of chicken soup and vegetables whose fresh colors and aromas could never be duplicated in the frozen-food or canned-goods sections of a supermarket. ''The philosophy of Jewish cooking is *'Ess! Ess!'* — 'Eat! Eat!' — and a lot of food is served. There are many courses, and large servings of many dishes, and the more you eat, the happier the Jewish cook is. It's an insult to leave anything over!

''On Friday nights, before the Sabbath, there is a big meal to get the family together, and also there are candles and a prayer. For an *hors d'ouevre* I would serve chopped liver on saltine crackers, and as an appetizer, *gefilte* fish with horse-radish on lettuce. Then, always, chicken soup. It is the Jewish cure-all! Any Jewish mother will give it to you if you have a cold, fever, virus, or any other sickness. And it is a delicious holiday soup, but then it must have *knaidlech, matzo* balls, in it to be complete. After the chicken soup, there is a tossed salad of about eight different vegetables, all fresh, with some simple dressing like lemon juice.

''Roast chicken with stuffing makes the main course, along with fresh peas and carrots, *challah,* which is a braided egg bread, and *kugel,* or noodle pudding. Wine, baked apple, tea, and sponge cake are the rest of the meal. The minute you're done with one course, the next is served; you don't even sit, because the minute your *gefilte* fish is gone, out comes the chicken soup.''

From sundown on Friday until twilight ends on Saturday, Jews who observe the Sabbath scrupulously don't work, buy, sell, use motors or electrical appliances, or indulge in sports, movies, parties, or other entertainment. Families keep the Sabbath with varying degrees of strictness, but the

warmth of the special meal on Friday evenings, with all the family members, old and young, gathered to celebrate their common heritage and solidarity, has left its imprint on nearly all Jews.

Passover, *Pesach,* also gathers the Jewish family together. Its *seder,* the order of service, is a joyful feast whose foods and rituals recall the Jews' miraculous escape from Egyptian slavery more than three thousand years ago. *Matzo,* unleavened bread, is eaten because the Jews fled Egypt so hastily they had no time to put yeast in their bread dough. *Moror,* bitter herbs, are a reminder of the bitterness of slavery; horseradish is the usual choice. A lamb shankbone symbolizes the lamb which was sacrificed and eaten at Passover in the days before the Temple in Jerusalem was destroyed. Other symbolic foods are roasted egg; *karpas,* which may be celery, parsley, or potatoes; and *charosis,* a mixture of fruit, nuts, cinnamon or ginger, and sweet wine.

The first part of the *seder* includes special prayers and blessings, and both ritual and impromptu questions from the children. Then comes the lavish meal itself, with special Passover dishes, glassware, and utensils, and the best foods and wines the family can buy. The house sparkles after its complete housecleaning, and not a particle of *chometz,* leaven, remains in it. The family, dressed in its best clothing, feels like royalty on Passover — and eats that way! Chicken, turkey, and duck appear in their most festive forms, vegetables are served in ingenious sauces, salads contain more kinds of vegetables than usual, and *kugel,* a noodle pudding, is sure to appear. There are not only the cracker-like *matzos* themselves, but a variety of dishes made either from *matzos* or from *matzo* meal: *knaidlech, matzo* balls, in the chicken soup; *matzo kugel; matzo*-meal *latkes,* pancakes; fried *matzos;* Passover *blintzes;* and any of a number of cakes made without leavening. After the closing psalms of praise and the final cup of wine, many families end the *seder* with the singing of Hebrew folk tunes.

On lesser occasions, chicken may appear in humbler, but no less tasty form, as Rae explains: ''Chicken in a brown bag with tons of garlic on it; that's the real way. First you wash it in boiling water. After that you stick garlic cloves into it, and rub it all over with garlic, a lot of it, and sprinkle it with paprika. Then you put it in a brown paper bag and stick it into an oven for an hour. That keeps all the juice and flavor in without getting the oven dirty.'' Then she adds, looking puzzled, ''But everyone makes chicken that way; people wouldn't be interested in hearing about that!''

Washing the chicken is a holdover from the *kosher* laws which were part of the Covenant made between God and the nation of Israel at Mount Sinai. *Kosher* means ''fit,'' not only hygienically, but ceremonially — all *kosher* food is highly sanitary, but not all wholesome food is *kosher.* In addition to specifying which animals may be eaten, the dietary laws prescribe a quick, painless slaughtering method which also reduces the amount of blood left in the meat. Housewives once washed and soaked their meat to supplement the precautions taken by the *shohet,* the slaughterer, but now *kosher* food is available already washed and soaked.

The *kosher* rule which sets Jewish cooking apart from that of all other peoples is the ban, mentioned in Exodus 23:18, on ''boiling a kid in its mother's milk.'' Strictly interpreted, it has meant that *milchiks,* dairy foods, could not be cooked or served with *flaishiks,* meat products, and even that separate sets of dishes and utensils had to be used for the two. Although holiday meals are traditionally based on meats, dairy meals can be almost as impressive. Rae says, ''We always had a dairy meal the evening before the Friday night meal, and often *blintzes* were the main dish. There are different fillings, such as pot cheese, which is very dry cottage cheese, or blueberries, apples, cheese, or any fruit or vegetable.'' *Blintzes* with meat fillings may also be served, if it is not a dairy meal, but then the batter should be based on chicken broth and not milk, in order to be *kosher.*

Rae's family came to New York City from Brest-Litovsk, Russia, in the late 1800s, and she speaks Yiddish as fluently as English. ''My father was a musician who also had a tobacco store,'' she says. "He came over to America because in Russia the Jewish people lived in ghettos and had no freedom, and my mother had six children to take care of. I married Nathan Keller; he was in the textile business, but then the Depression came and he lost his business, and shortly after that he died and I was left penniless, with two children. I took a job in a lace house, cutting out little patterns in the lace. Then after five years I borrowed money from the bank to pay a month's rent on a building, took out a license, and hired five women to cut lace into the patterns.''

By the time Rae retired in 1958, her lace factory was a 20-woman operation. Now she lives on the sixth floor of a brick apartment building in Brooklyn; she has lived in the same apartment 32 years. "I love it; it's my home," she says. "I know everybody. Somewhere I read that there are more Jewish people in Brooklyn than in Israel! If I go out for a walk, I know almost every single person and say 'Hello.' The little chairs are lined up outside on the nice days, and we all sit there and talk. We have two good delicatessens close by, that make their own pastrami and corned beef, and you can get honey-dipped pot roast, tongue, everything. And there are little vegetable stands outside the stores; I don't use canned vegetables.''

Asked where to get the sorrel grass to make *schav,* Rae looks surprised and says, "Anywhere; don't you have a Walbaum's near you?'' (If you don't, try substituting spinach.) And, like many Jewish cooks, Rae scorns written recipes and exact measurements: "I don't use measuring spoons or cups; I put it into my hand, and that is how I know. Jewish cooks cook from their heads; they cook by taste.'' The only way to get Rae's recipes was to take her "pinches'' and "little bits'' and put them in measuring spoons and cups, then write down the amounts. "I don't have any special philosophy of cooking,'' Rae adds. "I just cook. What makes a good cook? A good eater; that's what makes a good cook!''

"What makes a good cook?
A good eater; that's what makes
a good cook."

BORSHCH (BEET SOUP)

5 medium-size fresh beets,   2 eggs, beaten
  with their leaves and stems   juice of 1 1/2 lemons
2 to 3 quarts water   2 tablespoons sugar, or to taste
1 teaspoon salt, or to taste   1 cup sour cream

Scrub and peel beets. Wash stems and leaves with salt water to
remove dirt and insects. Cook beets, stems, and leaves in 2 to 3
quarts water until beets are done. Drain beets; save water. Grate
the cooked beets, after discarding stems and leaves; add lemon
juice, salt, and sugar. Return this mixture to the water in which
the beets were cooked. Let cool. Beat eggs well and add to cooled
soup. Bring soup to a boil; then chill. Serve topped with sour
cream, cucumber, and/or boiled potatoes. Serves about 8.

NO-FLOUR NUTCAKE

5 eggs, separated   1/2 pound ground hazelnuts
1 cup sugar   (1 pound unshelled)

Grind nuts until very fine in blender or in hand grinder or
grater. Cream sugar and egg yolks together. Beat egg whites until
they form firm peaks. Gradually fold nuts alternately with egg
whites into the yolk-and-sugar mixture. Bake in 9-inch springform
pan or a pan about 9 inches x 9 inches, greased and floured, for
about 55 minutes at 350 degrees. When cake is done, it is dry and
springs back when touched lightly with finger.

BLINTZES

BATTER
3 eggs, beaten   1/8 teaspoon salt
1/2 cup sifted flour   melted butter for greasing pan
1/2 cup milk, mixed with
  1/2 cup water

Beat eggs and salt together very well. Alternately add flour and
the milk-and-water mixture, little by little, beating after each
addition. Batter should be very smooth. Heat a 6-inch cast-iron

skillet over medium heat, and, using pastry brush, grease skillet lightly with melted butter. Use 1/4-cup-size measuring cup to pour batter into skillet until bottom is covered; pour off excess batter. Cook until batter looks dry and comes away from side of skillet. Invert skillet and whack it against a wooden board, so that the *blintze* falls out on the board with its fried side up. Repeat this process until the batter is used up, brushing the skillet with melted butter as needed. As each *blintze* is done, set it on waxed paper or a damp cloth.

FILLING

1/2 pound pot cheese	1 tablespoon sugar, or to taste
(*very* dry cottage cheese)	1 egg beaten
1/2 pound farmer's cheese	pinch of salt

Mix all ingredients together well. Put 1 tablespoon of filling in center of cooked side of each *blintze*. Fold one edge over to cover filling. Fold other edge to overlap first edge. Roll over with edges underneath, to close. With the edges still underneath, warm in buttered pan until lightly browned. Serve with sour cream, or with a mixture of sugar and cinnamon. For variety, add blueberries, strawberries, apples, or other favorite fruit. This recipe serves about 5 for a dairy-meal main dish.

GEHAKTE LEBER (CHOPPED LIVER)

1/2 pound chicken livers, broiled	1 large onion, chopped
2 hard-boiled eggs	*schmaltz* (chicken fat) or oil for frying onion
salt and pepper, to taste	

Brown chopped onion in *schmaltz* or oil. Grind hard-boiled eggs and broiled livers in meat grinder, or purée them in blender. Mix with browned onions and *schmaltz* or oil. Add salt and pepper. Mash well with fork until smooth, but not dry. If necessary, add more *schmaltz* or oil. Chill. Serve with crackers or on a bed of lettuce. Serves 4.

KUGEL (NOODLE PUDDING)

1/2 pound wide noodles,
  uncooked
3 eggs, beaten
1 medium onion, finely grated

2 tablespoons fat, melted
pinch each of salt and pepper,
  to taste

Boil and drain noodles. Add beaten eggs, melted fat, grated onion, salt, and pepper. Mix well. Put into a well-greased baking pan (about 8 inches x 8 inches) or a 1 1/2-quart casserole and bake at 425 degrees until noodles look brown and crispy on top, about 30 minutes. Serves 6.

SWEET KUGEL

1/2 pound wide uncooked
  egg noodles
3 eggs
1 1/2 teaspoons ground
  cinnamon

1/2 cup chopped walnuts
1 tablespoon melted fat
1 scant cup sugar
1 large apple, grated into strips
1/2 cup raisins (or currants)

Boil and drain noodles. Combine with melted fat, eggs, sugar-cinnamon mixture, apples, raisins, and nuts. Pour into well-greased, deep pudding dish (or baking pan about 8 inches x 8 inches) and bake at 425 degrees for about 30 minutes, or until noodles are brown on top. Serve hot or cold as a side dish instead of potatoes on holidays. Serves 6.

GEFILTE FISH

SOUP STOCK

3 medium onions, sliced
2 stalks celery, sliced

2 medium carrots, sliced
2 to 3 quarts water

FISH

1 1/2 pounds whitefish
3 medium onions, sliced
2 eggs
2 stalks celery
horseradish

1 1/2 pounds pike
1 carrot
1 teaspoon salt
1/2 teaspoon pepper

Fillet the whitefish and pike. Put bones and heads of fish into heavy pot with enough water to cover; add all other ingredients of soup stock. Cover, and bring to a boil. Meanwhile, grind the filleted fish, onions, carrots, and celery ("fish" ingredients); add eggs, salt, and pepper. Mix very well until all ingredients are blended evenly. Wet hands and form fish mixture into 10 to 12 patties. Drop them into the boiling soup stock and cook slowly for 2 hours, uncovered. Remove the fish from the stock and throw away the heads and bones. Refrigerate the fish patties and the stock separately until the stock congeals. Serve patties cold or warm with the stock, and with horseradish. Serves 5 to 6 people.

SCHAV (SOUR GRASS)

1 pound schav (sour grass*), or
substitute 1 pound fresh spinach
1 quart water
1 tablespoon sugar, or to taste
1 cup sour cream

1 teaspoon salt
1 beaten egg
green onions, as desired

Remove stems from schav and tie them up. Wash the leaves thoroughly. Put salt and sugar in water, bring to a boil, and boil stems, leaves, and chopped green onions about 15 minutes. Remove the stems. Let cool, and add beaten egg. Chill the schav and serve as a cold soup, with sour cream stirred in immediately before serving. Serves 6.

CHICKEN SOUP

3-to-4-pound chicken, cut up
1 large onion, cut up
2 stalks of celery, including
leaves, chopped
1 parsnip, peeled and cut up
1 to 2 tablespoons salt,
or to taste

3 to 4 quarts water, or
enough to cover chicken
2 medium carrots, scraped
and cut up
handful of uncooked baby
lima beans
7 or 8 sprigs of fresh dill

* Rumex acetosa and Rumex acetosella, called sheep sorrel or sour sorrel in some regions, are common North American weeds. To identify, see page 269 of Stalking the Blue-Eyed Scallop, by Euell Gibbons, Van Rees Press, 1964; or consult any wild plant guide or botany text.

Wash chicken and remove excess fat. Put into large kettle with water and all other ingredients except the dill. Cover and simmer until chicken is tender, about 1 1/2 hours. Remove chicken from soup and simmer soup, covered, 30 minutes longer. Remove from heat, add dill, cover, and let stand 30 minutes. Refrigerate soup. Skim fat off top of soup. Reheat and serve. Serves about 8.

MATZO BALLS

5 eggs, separated
1 teaspoon salt
1 1/2 tablespoons melted *schmaltz*
  (chicken fat)

1/8 teaspoon pepper
1 teaspoon cold water
1 cup *matzo* meal

Beat egg whites until stiff. Beat egg yolks until light yellow. Add water, salt, pepper, and *schmaltz* to beaten yolks; fold into the beaten egg whites. Fold in *matzo* meal gradually, a spoonful at a time. Refrigerate at least 1 hour. With hands wetted, shape dough into balls about the size of a walnut. Drop into rapidly boiling chicken soup. Reduce heat and simmer, covered, about 30 minutes. Serve in soup, or with poultry or a roast. Makes 12 *matzo* balls.

"I made my nephews be proud and speak Greek out loud in the streets."

GREEK

The Greeks have a saying that the best cooks are from the island of Crete, and Artemisia Callas has been proving it ever since she came to America as a bride in 1932. Bustling about a kitchen which looks ordinary, but smells irresistibly sweet and spicy, she deftly prepares everything from thick, foamy coffee and pastries for a visitor, to imposing feasts of stuffed grape leaves, roast lamb, cumin-spiced bread, and other delicacies for special family gatherings.

Fennel and mint from her own herb garden are drying on her dining room table. "They go in stuffed tomatoes," she explains, "and are good with greens. Put the mint, fennel, and tender squash leaves and blossoms in a pan with olive oil and their own water. Then add spinach and other greens, like tender leaves of chard, beet, and tomato. Don't add water, and cook over low heat; you never tasted anything better!"

The table also holds more than a dozen loaves of her fragrant homemade bread. "I make zwieback out of some of the bread," she says. "You can dip it in coffee, or put Greek jelly on it. In the morning I like it with a cup of coffee and a piece of cheese. In Greece, the villagers would always eat a big breakfast, but a city breakfast was small. When I came here I thought it was funny to have eggs at breakfast. And in Greece, pancakes and waffles were for dinner, another light meal. The big dinner is at noon."

In the winter Artemisia lived and attended school in Canea, Crete's capital city, but in the summer she lived in the village of Sfakopigadi, Oleander Well, where her father owned property. ''We had red, red Romaica grapes, for the Cretan wine, and white ones for white wine and eating,'' she recalls. ''Oranges were sold everyplace, and there was a very beautiful grove of oranges near the capital. Cretan ones are the most expensive, and it took me a long time to get used to the oranges here. There are thousands of olive trees on Crete, and the island is also famous for tobacco and raisins. And bay leaves! The mountains are full of all kinds of herbs, and in spring and summer there is a beautiful smell when you walk there. You just make a tea from them and drink it; everything is there. Greece has been blessed with hundreds of different herbs, and in winter you can make a hundred different teas.''

Crete is Kazantzakis country, and the island has also given the world the Renaissance artist El Greco, and Mikis Theodorakis, composer of the music for ''Zorba the Greek,'' which was filmed not far from Artemisia's village. Artemisia was eager to come to America with her husband Pete, but leaving her family was very hard. However, the parting was not final, and she has twice been back to visit them in Crete. Always proud of her heritage, she paid no attention when her American nephews scolded her for speaking Greek. ''I made my nephews be proud and speak it out loud in the street,'' she recalls with a laugh, ''and I made my kids learn it too. There is a Greek saying, 'The more languages, the more eyes!' '' Artemisia's and Pete's four children all speak Greek. The grandchildren too, as they bob in and out of the Callases' kitchen, are quick to heed her rapid-fire Greek commands to get out of the way of the rolling pin, or to quit raiding the *kourabiedes.*

In Greece, Christmas is the time for *kourabiedes,* shortbread cookies; *Christopsomo,* Christmas bread; and *loukomades,* honey puffs; however, gifts are not exchanged until January 1, Saint Basil's Day. Then a *Vasilopeta,* a Saint Basil's cake, is baked, often with a piece of money in it which brings the finder good luck for the coming year.

The peak holiday of the year, of course, is Easter. ''It's like the Fourth of July is here,'' says Artemisia. ''There are even fireworks. We have dyed Easter eggs too, but we make only red eggs, representing the blood of Christ. The first Easter dinner I made in America, 35 Greeks came, and one man cried because we had *pastitsio.* He said, 'I've never tasted it since my mother made it in Greece.' We always had guests for Easter and Christmas both. After dinner there was Greek dancing. The sheepherders would kill a lamb and barbecue it, and all the Greeks from miles around would get together.''

In Greece it is traditional to kill the Easter lamb, dye the eggs, and serve lentil soup on Holy Thursday. *Lambropsomo,* an Easter bread, is baked on Holy Friday, and on Saturday the lamb is roasted on an open-air spit. After the midnight church service, with its lighted candles and fireworks, a late supper breaks the Lenten fast. ''We have another 'Lent' of two weeks before August 15,'' Artemisia says. ''That is 'The Falling Asleep of the *Theotokos.'* *Theotokos* is our name for the Mother; it means the carrier or bearer of God. Even people who are not very religious believe you must keep this fast.''

The Greeks extend their veneration for the *Theotokos* to all mothers, who are so respected by their children, especially their sons, as to be considered almost sacred. Artemisia was only thirteen when her mother died, and she took over the cooking for her father, sister, and brothers. ''I learned the most from my mother. She would say, 'Bring the casserole, put a little bit of oil in it, bring an onion,' and so I was cooking from the age of seven or eight. But my father did the shopping; this was the custom. The ladies stayed home, because it would have been a scandal if they had gone to the market place.''

Along with a strong mother figure, the Greek family has an even stronger father, and although he shops, it would be unthinkable for him to help with the housework. ''Greek women are very picky about cleanliness,'' says Artemisia. ''In a Greek house the floor may be dirt, because they are very poor in the villages, but the house will be spotless. The walls are always whitewashed and very clean, and the fireplace is scrubbed. They used to cook in a fireplace, but now there is no more wood, and they use gas or even electric stoves.''

On Artemisia's kitchen shelf, next to the old wooden clock and copper cooking pots, are two mortar and pestle sets. The smaller one is for everyday use, but the large wooden set, as in every Greek kitchen, is for making only one thing: *skordalia,* a mayonnaise-like garlic spread. But Artemisia says she does not use hers anymore: ''In this country people did not like the garlic. The Greek immigrants in our mining town used to take the bus far away, to make it away from people! They french-fried squash, green peppers, eggplant, and all kinds of vegetables, and dipped them in the *skordalia.* But I remember once, three days after I ate it, I met a friend and kissed her, and she said, 'You ate *skordalia!* ' ''

According to Artemisia, Greeks not only like garlic, but consider it a health food. ''They believe garlic has a good effect on high blood pressure,'' she says, ''but that too much increases the white cells. It is believed to be good for a virus, too. For *skordalia* the garlic is ground fine, and then either dry bread or potato is added. I used bread because it is easier. Then you grind walnuts very fine, add a little olive oil and vinegar, and repeat this, working it until it is done.''

A less risky Cretan specialty is Greek coffee, which is much like Turkish. It is brewed one cup at a time in a little long-handled brass or copper pot, and the more the coffee foams, the better it is. Greek coffee may be bought already ground in specialty food stores, or it may be ground by hand in the brass coffee grinder, resembling a large peppermill, found in every Greek home. Gourmets claim that Greek coffee can be brewed to 36 different degrees of sweetness, and the amounts of sugar and coffee in Artemisia's recipe may be varied to suit individual tastes: add one heaping teaspoon coffee and one level teaspoon sugar to a half measuring cup of water. Bring to a boil, and then serve.

MOUSSAKA

MEAT SAUCE

2 pounds ground beef	salt and pepper, to taste
1 heaping tablespoon cumin	1 medium onion,
seed, freshly crushed between	finely chopped
pieces of paper towel with	about 2 cups water
rolling pin or knife handle	
2 tablespoons tomato paste	

Cook ground beef in heavy skillet (covered) until golden brown. Add onion and cook until onion is soft (about 10 minutes). Add freshly crushed cumin, salt, pepper, and tomato paste diluted in water. Let cook slowly until thickened, and begin preparing eggplant.

EGGPLANT
2 large eggplants
salt and pepper
flour
vegetable oil

Peel eggplants and cut into thin slices. Salt and pepper each slice, roll in flour, and fry in vegetable oil. When cooked, drain on paper towels. In baking pan, about 13 inches x 9 inches, spread half of the fried eggplant slices to cover bottom of pan. Spread meat mixture on top of eggplant, and cover meat mixture with remaining eggplant slices.

CREAM SAUCE

4 cups milk	1/2 cup plus 1 tablespoon flour
dash of salt	2 tablespoons butter
3 egg yolks	3/4 cup grated Romano cheese

In heavy saucepan, heat milk and flour, stirring constantly until it comes to a boil. Add butter and dash of salt and continue to stir. Cook 2 or 3 minutes and then remove saucepan from heat. Beat egg yolks and add them slowly to milk mixture, stirring thoroughly. When egg yolks are blended in, add cheese and mix well. Pour sauce over meat mixture and eggplant slices in baking pan. Cook at 350 degrees until sauce is golden brown, about 35 to 40 minutes. Serves 6.

KOURABIEDES (POWDERED-SUGAR BUTTER COOKIES)

2 cups unsalted or clarified
  butter
1/2 cup sugar
1 teaspoon baking powder
2 tablespoons brandy or cognac
1 cup ground almonds, blanched
  and slightly roasted in oven
5 cups (approximately) sifted
  cake flour

powdered sugar
2 egg yolks
2 teaspoons vanilla extract
2 tablespoons orange
  blossom water (optional)

Melt butter, let cool, then beat well. Add sugar and beat; then add egg yolks and beat well. Add vanilla extract, brandy, orange blossom water, and baking powder; mix well. Stir in almonds and flour. Knead to form a stiff dough. Shape into balls and flatten, or form into quarter-moon shapes. Place on greased cookie sheets and bake at 350 degrees about 20 minutes or until cookies are a light golden color. When cookies have cooled, remove from cookie sheets onto waxed paper and dust generously with powdered sugar (use strainer to avoid lumps). Makes 60 to 70 cookies.

YOGURT CAKE (COFFEE CAKE)

Sift together into a large mixing bowl:
4 1/2 cups sifted flour   3 teaspoons baking powder
1 teaspoon baking soda

Mix in 2 cups sugar, and then add the following four ingredients:
2 eggs   2 cups plain, unsweetened yogurt
1 cup soft butter   grated rind of 1 lemon

Mix well, and put batter into large (about 11 inches x 16 inches) greased, floured baking pan. Mix together and sprinkle over the batter:
1/2 cup slivered or ground almonds   1 teaspoon cinnamon
1/2 cup sugar

Sprinkle 4 tablespoons melted butter over cake and bake at 350 degrees about 45 minutes.

PASTITSIO (BAKED MACARONI
WITH GROUND MEAT)

MEAT SAUCE

1/4 cup butter	1 1/2 pounds lean ground beef
1/4 cup red dry wine	1 small onion, finely chopped
1/4 teaspoon cinnamon	salt and pepper, to taste
(or a bit less)	2 1/2 cups water
2 tablespoons tomato paste	

Melt butter in large skillet; cook ground beef in it until a golden brown color. Add wine and cook slowly until liquid is almost gone. Add onion and let cook until onion pieces are soft (about 10 minutes). Add tomato paste, diluted in the water, and salt, pepper, and cinnamon. Let cook slowly until sauce thickens.

MACARONI

1 pound dry macaroni	salt
1 cup grated Romano cheese	water

Boil macaroni in salted water till as done as desired. Drain; mix in meat sauce and cheese. Spread macaroni mixture into greased baking pan, about 11 inches x 15 inches. Prepare cream sauce:

5 cups milk	3/4 cup flour
dash of salt	1/4 cup butter
3 egg yolks	3/4 cup grated Romano cheese

Heat milk and flour in a heavy saucepan, stirring constantly until it begins to boil; add dash salt and butter, stirring continuously. Cook 2 or 3 minutes; remove saucepan from heat. Beat egg yolks and add slowly to milk mixture, stirring constantly. When eggs are completely blended in, stir in cheese and mix well.

Pour part of sauce over macaroni; shake pan so that sauce penetrates to bottom. Pour rest of sauce over macaroni. Bake at 350 degrees to 375 degrees about 40 minutes, or until sauce is golden brown. Cool slightly, cut into squares, and serve. Serves 8 to 10.

DOLMADES (STUFFED GRAPE LEAVES)

1 pound ground beef   1/8 teaspoon cinnamon
3/4 cup finely chopped parsley   3/4 cup uncooked rice
1/2 cup finely chopped fennel   1/2 medium onion, chopped
  (or 1 tablespoon dried)   salt and pepper, to taste
1/3 cup finely chopped mint   3/4 cup olive oil
  (or 3/4 tablespoon dried)
4 or 5 finely chopped green onions
chopped pulp of 6 medium tomatoes (cut almost through upper
  portion of each to leave "lid" attached, and lift "lid" to spoon
  out pulp and seeds; put pulp and seeds into colander and let
  liquid drain into ground beef filling mixture)
1/4 cup butter
1 cup water
grape leaves (if commercially prepared grape leaves are used, first
  put in saucepan with some water, bring to a boil, drain off
  water; if fresh leaves are used, they must be the kind with no
  fuzz on either side, and they should be boiled until tender, 5 to
  6 minutes, before use)

Mix together all ingredients except tomato shells, grape leaves, butter, and water. Fill tomato shells with part of the mixture, and place in a heavy-bottomed kettle or dutch oven, buttered or oiled to prevent sticking. Stuff grape leaves with remaining mixture, fold shut, and place between and on top of tomatoes. Place butter on top; add 1 cup water. Place an ovenproof plate or bowl cover on top of *dolmades* as a weight, then put a cover on kettle or dutch oven. Bring to a boil, then lower heat and cook 1 hour and 15 minutes, making sure it boils slowly entire time. As main dish, serves 6. As side dish, serves 12.

AVGOLEMONO SOUP (EGG-LEMON SOUP)

6 cups broth from a fat chicken   1/2 cup uncooked rice
3 eggs, beaten   juice of half a medium-size
salt and pepper, to taste   lemon, strained

Boil rice in chicken broth with salt and pepper. When rice is cooked, lower heat to simmer setting. In a large mixing bowl, beat eggs well, add lemon juice slowly, and beat again. Add about 2 cups hot broth to egg *slowly*, continue beating, and then pour this egg mixture back into the pot, stirring well. Remove from heat at once so that eggs do not curdle. Serves 6 to 8.

BAKLAVA (GROUND NUT PASTRY)

1 1/2 pounds ground walnuts (or partly almonds)
1 cup ground zwieback
1 teaspoon cinnamon

2 tablespoons sugar
1 pound pastry sheets or *fillo*
melted butter (about 1 cup)

Mix walnuts, zwieback, cinnamon, and sugar. Place 5 or 6 sheets of pastry, each one buttered with a pastry brush, in an 11 inch x 14 inch baking pan. Spread about 1/3 of nut mixture on top, add 3 buttered pastry sheets, then another 1/3 of nut mixture, then 3 more buttered pastry sheets and rest of nut mixture. Top with 5 or 6 more individually buttered pastry sheets. Cut into diamond shapes with sharp knife before baking (and place one clove in middle of each diamond, if you wish). Bake at 325 degrees for about 1 hour or until golden brown. When cool, pour over *baklava* a hot syrup made as follows:

2 cups water
1/2 cup honey

1 1/2 cups sugar

Boil sugar and water slowly for at least 10 minutes, add honey, stir to blend, and bring to a boil again. Pour over *baklava* while syrup is still hot, or, if syrup has cooled, the *baklava* should be hot. Either the syrup or the *baklava* must be hot during pouring. Makes about 60 diamond pastries.

SPANAKORIZO (SPINACH AND RICE CASSEROLE)

1/3 cup olive oil
2 pounds fresh spinach, washed, drained, and chopped coarsely
1 small onion, chopped

salt and pepper, to taste
1 tablespoon chopped parsley
1 cup uncooked rice

1 tablespoon tomato paste, diluted
    in 1 1/2 to 2 cups water, depending
    on how much water clings to
    the spinach (optional)

Cover bottom of heavy, medium-size kettle with olive oil. Put in onion and parsley, then coarsely chopped spinach, salt, and pepper; simmer until spinach is as done as desired. Add rice and diluted tomato paste and enough additional water to cook rice. Bring to a boil and simmer about 20 minutes, until rice is cooked. As main dish, serves 5. As side dish, serves 8.

ITALIAN

"I showed them how to make *spaghetti* . . .," says 89-year-old Nellie Cito proudly, "and they know me everywhere. I cooked for the Grange and the church, and when we had a big *spaghetti* dinner for the PTA, they came to my house and wanted to know how. It was just a dab of this and a dab of that — and we served about 300! I made my own *pasta,* and had the machine to cut it.

"We were poor," Nellie recalls. "Everything we had, we had to raise ourselves, and we just cooked plain things on the farm. We never bought anything. We did our own canning, and had a cellar with shelves holding three or four hundred jars of everything — fruit, vegetables, crabapple jelly, peppers in vinegar. We butchered our own meat, three and four hogs a year, made sausage, and cured our own hams and bacon. There was a root cellar made of cement, with shelves around it, and a milk-house on top of it. We made our own butter, and had a separate place to hang the cheese, where it would drip. There were big barrels with brine for the pickles, and then a separate laundry-house, with a place to heat the water."

Nellie's father, Tony Dilemma, came to America from Esirnia, a village near Naples. Then when Nellie was four-and-a-half, she and her brother and mother joined him here: "My dad took the homestead first, and then my husband, Angelo, and I had it; our deed was signed by William Howard Taft. We came out of a town onto a prairie right on top of this hill, when nobody was there, just coyotes. My Tony was the first boy born on Gunbarrel Hill. My dad and husband were coal miners and didn't know a thing about farming; they were just as green as greenhorns.

"In Esirnia they had fruit trees, figs, peaches, pears, all kinds of grapes for wine. It never snowed there, and there were vegetables and fruit the year round. They had olives

and made their own oil, and had rooms and rooms of grapes
hanging up. My dad said he used to tromp the grapes with
his feet, and I said, 'Oh, I could never drink wine that had
been done that way.' But he explained they soaked their feet
clean in water first and said, 'The feet were cleaner than
your hands!' My mother said in the old country they never
tasted coffee but always had wine. You could take a bath in
wine, they had so much. The only time they had coffee was
when they were sick.

"My mother just cooked; she never measured anything.
And she made the best pies and cakes. She kept nine or ten
Italian miners as boarders all the time, and worked awfully
hard, even fixing them dinner pails. I never went to school
half the time because I had to help her. Angelo boarded there,
and my mother picked him out for my husband, and it
worked out all right."

How well it worked out was seen in 1948, when more
than 150 friends and relatives helped the Citos celebrate
their 50th wedding anniversary. Present were not only four
sons and three daughters, but also Nellie's father, tough and
enduring as the gnarled olive trees of his native Campania.
"He lived to be 97 or 98," says Nellie. "In his nineties he
was still climbing up in trees to prune them, and he dug a
tree just three days before he died."

Toughness and a boundless energy are still the marks of
the Citos, along with thick curly hair and a flair for cooking.
Nellie's daughter Flo and her husband ran an Italian
restaurant for many years, and their son is a partner in a
Mexican restaurant, while Nellie's daughter-in-law Lucille
upholds old-country traditions at an Italian restaurant,
cooking *pasta, pizza, ravioli, minestrone,* and other
Neapolitan dishes which to many Americans typify all
Italian cooking.

Actually, there is no one Italian cuisine; each province
and major city has its own characteristic wines, cheeses,
recipes, and preferences. Naples, in the south of Italy
between Rome and the "toe of the boot," bases its cooking
on olive oil, but in the north, where the climate is less

hospitable to olive trees, butter takes its place. Florence is famous for mushrooms; Genoa for its *pesto*-flavored *minestrone;* Venice for *scampi,* shrimps; and Rome for a wonderful golden wine named *Est! Est!! Est!!!* — a triple exclamation of "This is it!"

In Naples, the *pizza,* once considered strictly a peasants' dish, has the place of honor on the menu. *Pizza alla marinara,* reputed to be the ancestor of all *pizzas,* has a very simple topping of tomato purée, crushed garlic, and powdered marjoram, but its variations are endless. One of the most famous is *pizza Margherita,* invented in 1889 for the Italian queen of that name. It owes its distinctive flavor to finely chopped fresh basil, and to *mozzarella,* a soft cheese made, in Naples at least, from the milk of the *bufala,* the water buffalo.

As in many countries, the Christmas Eve dinner in Italy is traditionally fish, but the dish popular in Nellie's family, squid stuffed with chestnut dressing, has an unmistakable regional flavor. Christmas is also the signal for Flo's *scarpelle,* rosemary-flavored doughnuts containing mashed potatoes. At Easter there is the glory of her *shadone,* a lattice-topped pie with a filling blended of ham, cheese, and eggs.

Saints' days abound in Italy. Roast pork is eaten on Saint John's Day, and on the feast of Saint Honoré, patron saint of bakers, there is the elaborate *gato San Honoré,* an imposing edifice of cream puffs on a round base, with a fruit-topped, whipped-cream filling. On March 19, the feast of *San Giuseppe,* a long table is set up in the church square in small villages, and everyone puts a contribution of food on it. A man, woman, and child enacting the Holy Family sit at the head of the table, and widows, orphans, and the poor sit down as their guests. When the eating, drinking, and dancing are over, and the bonfire has subsided into embers, everyone takes Saint Joseph cookies home with him.

Although coffee was never important in Nellie's kitchen, it has been savored by Italians ever since the first European coffee house opened in Rome in 1615. It was the Italians who

invented *espresso,* a new method of brewing this beverage by passing a steam jet through very finely ground coffee. Small *espresso* coffeemakers are manufactured for home use, but the ultimate *espresso* machine is an imposing metal dome like the three-and-a-half-foot-high giant which dominates the dining room of the restaurant where Lucille cooks. A complicated array of levers and spouts studs its sides, and perched at the top is a gleaming metal eagle, supremely indifferent to the waitresses who expertly whisk cups of coffee from the machine in a variety of forms — black, topped with frothy, steam-heated milk to make *cappuccino,* or with cream or whipped cream. The metal eagle is of a species which seems doomed to extinction: no one makes these giant urns any more.

Spaghetti- makers, however, are another matter. Nellie's, patented in 1900, does not look much different from its gleaming modern descendents, although Nellie insists there is a difference: "My old *spaghetti-* maker has different rollers grooved for different sizes of *spaghetti — vermicelli* for soup, a medium size, and finger-width. You can't buy them any more, they're too old, and the new ones don't have all these gadgets." The handcranked machine flattens the *pasta* dough into smooth, elastic strips, working like the wringer on an old washing machine, and then the cutting attachment turns the dough into ribbons of *pasta.* Of course, the dough may instead be cut by hand after it has been rolled out: the piece of dough is rolled up like a jelly roll and sliced, and then each slice unrolls into a long noodle.

Nellie still likes to recall the old days: "I used to cook for the harvesters, and run the horse and wagon for the grain. I made the bread dough, went out and got a load of grain, and then when I came back, I pushed down the bread and stirred the soup. Then I got back on the wagon for another trip, carrying one kid and leading another by the hand, and leading the horse. It was the happiest time of my life!"

"Everything we had, we
had to raise ourselves."

PASTA

4 eggs   not quite 1/2 teaspoon salt
2 cups unsifted flour   water, as needed

Beat eggs, and gradually stir in the flour. Keep stirring until dough gets too thick for the spoon. Continue to add flour while kneading dough with hands. If you have a *spaghetti*-maker, divide dough into 3 or 4 parts, and feed them through the machine's smooth rollers one at a time. As each part comes out, fold it in thirds and feed through again, repeating this several times, and dusting *pasta* with flour if it seems sticky. The rollers should be set closer and closer together each time, and the machine should lengthen a 4-inch strip to about 12 inches. Set up the machine with a fine, medium, or wide cutter and feed 12-inch lengths of *pasta* through. If the dough is too hard to work, add a little water. Put finished ribbons of *pasta* on floured waxed paper; let *pasta* dry about 30 minutes. If you do not have a *spaghetti*-maker, knead dough on a floured board until it is elastic, 10 to 12 minutes. Divide it into 3 or 4 parts and roll them out into long rectangular strips one at a time on a floured board, until each part is about 4 inches wide, and 1/16 to 1/8 inch thick. Cutting the rectangles into 12-inch lengths, loosely roll each up from the narrow end, like a jelly roll. Cut in 1/4-inch-wide strips for regular noodles. For *lasagne* noodles, roll up 5-inch lengths and cut into strips 1 1/2 inches wide. Let dry on floured waxed paper about 30 minutes. Boil *pasta* 5 minutes in salted water (homemade *pasta* needs less cooking time than commercial) drain in a colander, and serve hot with butter or grated Parmesan cheese or sauce. Serves about 4 (in general, allow 1/4 pound of *pasta* per person).

MINESTRONE (ITALIAN SOUP)

4 to 6 quarts water   2 cups canned whole tomatoes,
1 to 2 tablespoons salt   or more, to taste
7 handfuls dry pinto beans   1 1/2 pounds bulk pork sausage
   (about 1 pound)   1/2 pound bacon ends or pieces
2 cups chopped celery   2 cups chopped onions
large package frozen or fresh   handful of dry basil
   zucchini, about 2 cups   (about 1/2 cup)

2 cups red Burgundy wine
2 cups cooked *pasta* (small
  macaroni, broken *spaghetti,*
  or homemade noodles)
2 handfuls dry beef stock
  (about 1 cup)

2 tablespoons garlic powder
1/3 head of cabbage, cut up
1/2 pound ground beef
2 handfuls grated Romano
  cheese (about 1 cup)

Boil dry beef stock, garlic powder, and pinto beans in the water. Squeeze tomatoes with hands and add, along with chopped celery, cabbage, and zucchini. Fry pork sausage, ground beef, and bacon pieces in a large frying pan. Chop onions and fry with meat. When meat and onions are browned, add them to the other ingredients in the soup kettle, and cook until beans are done, 2 to 3 hours. It is better to cook the *minestrone* all day. A few minutes before soup is done, add basil, grated Romano cheese, and red Burgundy. Immediately before serving, add cooked *pasta.* Serve hot, and put a shaker of grated Italian cheese on the table for those who want more. *Minestrone* can be refrigerated or frozen, and it always tastes better the second day than when freshly made. Makes 4 to 6 quarts of soup.

SCARPELLE (ITALIAN "DOUGHNUTS")

4 eggs, beaten
1/2 cup butter, melted
3 packages dry yeast *
1/2 cup sugar
4 cups sifted flour (about)
oil for deep-fat frying
1 to 2 teaspoons salt

2 cups cooked mashed potatoes
  (2 large potatoes)
2 cups lukewarm water from
  cooking potatoes, with 1/2 cup
  set aside
pinch of rosemary

Dissolve yeast in 1/2 cup lukewarm potato water. Add salt, sugar, melted butter, beaten eggs, mashed potatoes, and rest of water. Mix. Gradually add flour until the dough can be worked, but is still soft. Knead briefly, cover, put in a warm place, and let rise 2 hours, until about doubled in bulk. On a floured board, roll out dough about 1/3 inch thick, and cut into doughnut shapes with knife. (If you use a 3-inch doughnut cutter, you must keep

---

* 2 packages in the original recipe used at 5,200-foot altitude

flouring the cutter, and this extra flour is bad for the quality of the *scarpelle*.) Let rise on board or floured cookie sheet 30 to 45 minutes in a warm place, until doubled. Heat 2 to 3 inches of oil in kettle or deep-fat fryer to 375 degrees. Sprinkle rosemary in oil. Drop in *scarpelle*, but not so many that they are crowded. Fry until golden brown on both sides, turning once. (This takes 3 to 4 minutes if the oil is at proper temperature.) Drain *scarpelle* on paper towels and serve hot. Serve plain if used as the bread for the menu. Serve sprinkled with sugar-and-cinnamon mixture if used as a sweet. Makes about 40 *scarpelle*.

SHADONE (HAM AND CHEESE PIE)

DOUGH

10 cups sifted flour (about)
1 heaping tablespoon sugar
1 teaspoon salt
1 1/2 to 2 teaspoons baking
  powder*

1 1/2 cups shortening
1 tablespoon vanilla extract
6 eggs, beaten
1 1/2 cups milk

FILLING

12 eggs
1/2 teaspoon pepper
1/2 teaspoon nutmeg
1/2 cup "basket cheese"
  (undried cheese)
1 pound grated Romano cheese
1/2 to 1 cup raisins or
  currants (optional)

3 tablespoons sugar
3 large ham slices, diced
  (or cooked sausage)
1 tablespoon vanilla extract
1 pound grated Swiss cheese
a pinch of basil

GLAZE

1 egg, beaten with a little sugar and salt

Sift flour, sugar, salt, and baking powder together. Cut in the shortening as for pie dough. Mix in vanilla extract, beaten eggs, and milk to form a soft dough. Knead briefly, and divide into 2 parts. Roll out 1 part into a rectangle about 1/8 inch thick. Line a large baking pan (about 10 inches x 14 inches x 2 inches) with the

---

* 1 teaspoon is used in the original recipe at 5,200-foot altitude

dough, leaving a little hanging over the edges (or divide dough into 4 parts and use 2 smaller baking pans). Mix filling ingredients together well and spread over dough in pan. Roll out other half of dough 1/8 inch thick, cut into strips, and make a lattice to go on top of the filling, crimping it to the bottom part of the dough. Brush with the glaze, and bake at 350 degrees until dough is nice and brown, about 1 hour. The *shadone* can be frozen, and then thawed before it is cooked.

PIZELLE (THIN CRISP COOKIES)

8 eggs, well beaten
2 cups sugar
1 cup butter, melted
1 teaspoon salt

1/3 cup liquid anise or vanilla
  extract, or to taste
4 or more cups flour, sifted
pizelle iron or *cialde* iron

Beat the eggs, add the sugar, and beat well. Continue to beat while adding melted butter, salt, vanilla extract, and anise extract, and blend evenly. (If you do not continue beating, the melted butter may cook the eggs.) Gradually stir in sifted flour, with less flour for crisper cookies, and more flour for thicker cookies. Heat cookie iron over burner until a drop of water sizzles on it. Dab a generous teaspoonful of batter in center of one side of iron. Press sides of iron shut and cook, turning frequently from one side to the other, and opening sides to look at cookie, until it is a golden brown. Makes 55 to 60 cookies about 5 inches in diameter.

SPAGHETTI SAUCE AND MEATBALLS

SAUCE

two 15-ounce cans tomato
  purée
salad oil for frying
28-ounce can tomatoes
two or three 15-ounce cans
  of water
two 8-ounce cans tomato
  paste
1/2 teaspoon sugar
2 or 3 pork blades

1 tablespoon minced onion,
  or to taste
1 tablespoon grated Parmesan
  cheese, or to taste
salt, pepper, basil,
  and parsley, to taste
1 tablespoon garlic powder,
  or to taste
1 tablespoon oregano,
  or to taste

Heat oil in pan. Add tomato purée and tomato paste, and then dilute with 2 or 3 cans (15-ounce) of water. Add sugar, salt, pepper, basil, parsley, garlic, tomatoes, onion, oregano, and Parmesan cheese. In another pan, brown the pork blades. Put browned pork blades in with sauce. Cook at least 3 to 4 hours, adding water as needed. If you do not need the full recipe, freeze what is left over.

MEATBALLS

3 pounds ground beef	1 pound ground pork
2 eggs	1/4 pound bread crumbs
1/2 clove garlic, crushed	(may soak them in water)
a little basil	a little parsley
1 tomato, puréed	1/2 cup grated Romano cheese

Mix beef and pork. Add eggs and mix. Crush garlic and add, along with parsley, basil, bread crumbs, and grated Romano cheese. When mixture is evenly blended, form it into hard, solid balls about 1 inch in diameter. Put meatballs in saucepan, top with tomato, cover with lid, and simmer very slowly so that meatballs do not stick to the bottom. No cooking oil is needed; the pork makes its own grease. Turn meatballs with spatula, and do not let them get too brown. Add meatballs to *spaghetti* sauce only about 30 minutes before the sauce is done, so that the meatballs do not cook too long and fall apart.

CZECHOSLOVAKIAN

Soup stock simmers merrily in the pot on the stove, and Barbara Trousil's fingers are swift and sure as she prepares *knedlíky*, dumplings, and drops them into the rich broth. These are liver dumplings, but in her native Czechoslovakia, where dumplings appear at almost every meal, there are innumerable kinds and sizes: bread dumplings shaped in long rolls; rice dumplings; dessert dumplings of cottage cheese, filled with fruit or jam; Cream of Wheat dumplings; sauerkraut dumplings; and hearty potato dumplings the size of tennis balls.

"It should be fresh-ground pepper in the liver dumpling mix," says Barbara. "The garlic is cut very fine, then mashed with salt with the tip of the knife. Put a little water in the saucer to set the dumplings in, and wet your hands to form them. If they fall apart, wet your hands more. You can make the mix a day ahead; put the dumplings in a pan with a little water in it in the refrigerator, not covered. And I always have the oxtail stock at home, and maybe put in chicken backs. I made thousands and thousands of these dumplings for ten years in my carry-out food kitchen in Chicago. The soup was 75¢ a quart, and every Sunday I had a line of people for it."

Barbara had come to the United States in the twenties, but in the thirties she returned to Czechoslovakia with her husband, a chemist. "In 1946 I came back to Chicago to renew my citizenship," Barbara says. "While I was here my husband died in Czechoslovakia, and my twin sons came here too. They said, 'Mother, here is the money we have; do whatever you want with this money.' I invested it in an American-Bohemian kitchen and advertised, and soon I had a cook, and a man to cut and serve meat, and a woman for fish, and a salesgirl. I had apple *strudel* at the kitchen only Saturday.''

Barbara is very proud of her sons, who are both chemists, and their families: ''I think Robert and Eddie grew so big because we never bought prepared baby food. My husband used to be so particular, and every day he told me a different menu for the children. You never saw such healthy, beautiful children as in Prague, because of how they ate. They would mash cooked carrots with the skin on for the children, and do this with every vegetable. As soon as the mother saw the baby did not have enough by nursing, she would boil butter till it was clear, and then put in flour and fry it till it was pink, because that is a lot of dextrose. And we gathered rose hips and made a jelly from them; miles of wild rose hips were planted along the roads for the people. There was a certain machine to mash the hips, and the juice went one way, the rest the other way. It's the fruit with the most vitamin C; my children were raised on vitamin C. We still travel to New Mexico for a week, the whole family, and pick so many rose hips, and then make the good jelly from them.''

Barbara grew up near Prague, in what was once Bohemia, or *Čechy,* the Czech lands. Mozart lived and worked in *Zlatá Praha,* golden Prague, and it is also the city of the tenth century martyr Saint Vaclav, better known as Good King Wenceslas.

''The mountain country is beautiful,'' says Barbara. ''We had three castles near us, and it used to be three miles from our village to the church which is famous for kings and counts. When they came down to hunt, they had seats by the altar, but we always thought the counts were ugly. They did not live so healthy a life as we did. There were eleven of us children, and we were so healthy. Once a week we had meat, just a small piece of meat. First we would make soup of it, then gravy of it, onion gravy. All Czech cooking is good cooking, and tasty, because we take time to make it. Another thing is, in Czechoslovakia we never eat any meal without soup. My first love is tripe soup, and you can still hear Czech people say it's good after too much partying. What wonderful spinach soup we have! And you don't have to have beef; people should know how wonderful *řízky* are, pork *Wiener Schnitzels,* and the meat is not very expensive. You cut pork thin, and pound it to make it thinner. You dip it in an egg-and-flour mixture, then corn crumbs, and fry; people should know what a wonderful meal this is.

"On our Thanksgiving, which is earlier than here, October 28, Czechs have roast goose, liver dumpling soup, sauerkraut, dumplings, and apple strudel. Lots of people eat raw sauerkraut; it is so delicious. You've got to know how to prepare it. We put in onion, cut very fine, and a tiny bit of olive oil, lemon juice, pepper, and sugar and salt. And you never rinse it, ever! It's a big mistake to rinse it; you rinse the good out of it. And this makes it sweet and sour.

"Thanksgiving is two days," Barbara continues. "The first day you go to church, and the second day you dance, and maybe another day after that. And people won't think they are having Thanksgiving without *klobásy,* sausages. To make them you take lean veal and lean pork, half and half, and grate in finely cut onions, garlic, and pepper that is pounded, not ground. You mix this with dry white wine, and a very few bread crumbs to hold it together. People were so particular that they baked bread especially for these bread crumbs. Then with a machine you put it in the casings, half a yard long, and tie the casings in spirals. You put a little piece of special sharp wood, a skewer, in the sausage to hold it together, and then they are fried in wine. This is the best thing out of the whole world! And that rye bread they bake is round and flat, baked very slowly, and thick and crisp. It is most important for it to be crisp. They don't make fancy sweet bread; bread should be bread!"

In Prague, frankfurters are called *párky,* pairs, because they are always sold in twos, and they are sold hot and ready to eat in special sausage shops. The city is famous for its many varieties of sausage, Prague ham, and beer halls. Czech beer, especially Pilsner, is considered the best in the world by many, and certainly by Barbara: "That's the best beer; you never get tired of it. All others are artificial compared to it!" She is also loyal to Czech potatoes: "People there live on potatoes, and they're better ones than here. The only ones I use here are Idaho potatoes, because they have less water in them."

Before opening her carry-out kitchen, Barbara had cooked extensively for restaurants and individual families: "It's easy to cook for rich people, because they buy the best meat; oh, how I know how to cook the wild ducks. And it's easy to do pork crown roast; that's the best pork you can make, with apples, and cooked in ginger ale. Chocolate wine cake is my real secret, but I was also very famous for a nut torte made from fresh hazelnuts. That's our Czech favorite. It has whipping cream in the middle, and you use only Holland chocolate for it. I made it only for special people in Palm Springs, and I did not give the recipe until I left there!

"If you have a little bit of an idea about cooking, you don't have to be afraid to cook any kind of meal. Only you have to have a little talent, not only to cook, but new ideas about how to serve it. One of my ideas was to take a little piece of toast, and butter one side, because otherwise it would shrink. Then I put a little onion ring, mayonnaise, and sliced cucumber, and put caviar on. They were crazy about it!"

"If you have a little bit of an idea about cooking, you don't have to be afraid to cook. . . ."

TAŽENY JABLKOVÝ ZÁVIN
(CZECH STRETCHED STRUDEL)

DOUGH

1 1/2 cups sifted flour, plus about 1/2 cup
1/4 teaspoon salt
1 egg

1/2 cup warm water
1 teaspoon melted butter
brandy to sprinkle on dough

Sift 1 1/2 cups of flour and 1/4 teaspoon salt together into bowl, and make a well in the center. Mix water, egg, and melted butter; pour into well, and slowly work mixture into the flour. Then knead on a floured board, adding flour as needed, until dough does not stick to hands, and is elastic (about 20 minutes). Put dough on plate, moisten outside with a little butter to keep it from cracking, cover with a cloth, and let stand about 1 hour in a warm place. Flour the dough and put it on a floured pastry paper or cloth. With a floured rolling pin, roll the dough into as large a circle as possible, about 15 inches across. Then butter your hands and start to pull from the middle until the dough is about double in diameter, lifting the edge with both hands and stretching it by pulling hands apart, and moving hands farther along the edge and repeating the process. When properly stretched, the dough will be paper-thin. Let circle of dough stand 30 minutes to dry slightly, and do not touch it. Melted butter, or preferably brandy, may be brushed on the dough.

FILLING

1/2 cup butter, melted
3/4 cup toasted bread crumbs
  (or 3/4 cup cornflake crumbs)
1 cup sugar mixed with
  1 teaspoon ground cinnamon
1 cup or less raisins or currants

about 4 pounds pie apples, peeled, cored, and sliced *
1/2 cup chopped almonds or other nuts

Brush dough with 1/2 of melted butter. Covering 1/2 to 3/4 of the dough to within 1 to 2 inches from edges, sprinkle dough in alternating layers of the crumbs, apples, cinnamon-sugar mixture, raisins or currants, nuts, and the rest of the melted butter. Cut off thickened edges of dough and roll up *strudel* by gently lifting cloth

* If apples are too sweet, add 1/2 cup lemon juice.

or paper. Transfer to greased cookie sheet, crimping edges shut, and curving *strudel* to fit sheet. Bake at 400 degrees about 20 minutes; then reduce heat to 300 degrees and bake about 30 minutes more, or until golden brown. Makes one 3-foot *strudel* or two 1 1/2-foot *strudels*.

HOUSKOVÉ KNEDLÍKY (BREAD DUMPLINGS)

1 cup milk at room temperature   1/2 package dry yeast
1 cup water   1 tablespoon salt
2 eggs   3 slices white bread, in
5 cups sifted flour   toasted crouton-like squares

Dissolve yeast in milk. Mix with water, salt, and beaten eggs. Stir in sifted flour, beat well, and knead lightly to form a dough. Fold bread squares into mixture; let stand about 30 minutes. Divide dough into 4 parts and form each into a long roll about 2 inches in diameter. Cook dumplings, covered, in boiling salted water about 20 minutes. Remove and drain on paper towels. While still hot, cut into slices with a thread, and serve with *svíčková* or other meat dish that is accompanied by gravy or sauce.

BRAMBOROVÉ KNEDLÍKY (POTATO DUMPLINGS)

2 large white potatoes, boiled   2 egg yolks
   and peeled   1 tablespoon farina-type cereal
1 cup sifted flour   (such as Cream of Wheat)
1 teaspoon salt
about 6 tablespoons croutons,
   or bacon, ham, or
   any leftover meat

While potatoes are still hot, mash until very fine. Beat in 2 egg yolks, teaspoon of salt, and cereal. Let cool. When ready to cook, mix in 1 cup sifted flour and make dough. Form dough into 6 balls; in the middle of each, put a tablespoon of croutons, or bacon, ham, or other meat. Drop into boiling salted water and simmer, covered, about 10 to 15 minutes, or until dumplings rise to surface. Serve hot. Makes 6 dumplings.

OLD-FASHIONED BAKED WILD DUCKS

5 or 6 wild ducks, cleaned,   1 cup buttermilk
  plucked, heads and feet cut off,   1 pound unsalted, uncooked
  oil sac at base of tail removed   slab bacon
6 cups red Port wine   3 apples, peeled, cored,
2 bay leaves   and halved
2 or 3 teaspoons thyme, to taste
3 to 6 cups cooked wild rice

Wash ducks thoroughly, inside and out. Marinate 24 hours in mixture of red Port wine, buttermilk, and bay leaves. Remove ducks and save marinade. Rub ducks inside and out with thyme. Cut bacon into thin strips and, making openings in duck skins with a knife, slide bacon strips in under skins as much as possible.* Stuff each duck with about 1/2 to 1 cup wild rice and 1/2 apple. Place ducks on rack in roasting pan, cover with more strips of bacon, and pour in marinade. Cover pan and bake at 300 degrees for 1 1/2 hours. Baste ducks with marinade every 15 minutes. Take cover off and brown ducks under broiler for 5 minutes or less. Return ducks to oven and spoon juice glaze over them from pan.

GLAZE
1 pint orange juice
finely grated peel of 1 orange

Increase oven temperature to 500 degrees. Glaze ducks with above mixture every 3 minutes for about 10 minutes, until nice and shiny. Take out of oven and keep hot until ready to serve. Serves 6 to 8.

ČERVENY ZELÍ (SWEET-SOUR CABBAGE)

1 small red cabbage,   1/2 cup chopped onion
  very finely cut up   1/4 cup vinegar
4 cups water   salt, pepper, and sugar, to taste

* It helps to use a larding needle (a large curved needle available in hardware stores) to force the bacon under the skin.

1 teaspoon salt   2 tablespoons flour
bacon fat for frying   3 tablespoons brown sugar

Simmer cabbage in water about 30 minutes, until done but still a little crisp. Fry chopped onion in bacon fat. Add flour to fat and pour in some of the liquid in which the cabbage was cooked. Add vinegar and brown sugar, and then mix everything together. Season to taste with salt, pepper, and sugar. Serves about 6.

SVÍČKOVÁ (MARINATED BEEF)

2-to-3-pound piece of lean   12 whole peppercorns
  beef, elk, or venison   8 whole allspice
1/2 cup celery root, sliced   2 juniper berries (optional)
  (optional)   salt and pepper, to taste
1 cup onion, sliced   2 slices of lemon peel
2 bay leaves
1/2 teaspoon thyme
Chianti wine, enough to cover vegetables
    (or 1/2 vinegar, 1/2 water)
1/4 pound sliced bacon, uncooked
1/2 cup carrots, cut up
1/2 cup parsley root, sliced
    (or substitute 1/2 cup sliced parsnip)

Mix all ingredients together except meat and Chianti. Cover these mixed ingredients with Chianti, put in a pot, and simmer until they reach the boling point. Remove from heat and let cool. Wash and dry the meat. Pour the cooled marinade over the meat and let stand 2 to 3 days, turning with spoons once a day. Line a baking dish with uncooked bacon slices. Put the meat and marinade in on top of the bacon. Bake uncovered in 350-degree oven 3 hours or more, until well done, basting frequently. When it is done, work the gravy and vegetables through a cone-shaped sieve with a wooden pestle, or through an ordinary sieve.

THICKENING MIXTURE
1 pint sour cream   4 tablespoons flour
2 to 3 tablespoons sugar   1 tablespoon lemon juice, or to taste
a little water   1 tablespoon butter

After gravy and vegetables are sieved, thicken with mixture of sour cream and flour. In a heavy pan over low heat, melt sugar and butter to a dark brown syrup, stirring constantly, and as soon as done, add enough water to cool it. Add to gravy, along with lemon juice. Serve meat and marinade with dumplings. Serves about 8.

CZECH NUT TORTE

CAKE LAYERS

3 cups grated nutmeats, sifted and well packed
10 eggs, separated
1/4 cup Dröste cocoa (no other brand)
1/2 cup brewed coffee
1 1/4 cups sugar
1 teaspoon vanilla extract
1/2 cup grated vanilla-cookie crumbs

Grease three 10-inch layer cake pans with butter and dust them with flour. Beat 10 egg yolks until they are light lemon color. Add sugar slowly and mix in. Add vanilla extract and mix in. Make a paste from the brewed coffee and the cocoa powder; add paste to the egg-yolk mixture. Then add 3 cups finely grated nuts to this mixture. Add the cookie crumbs and mix in. Fold in 10 egg whites which have been beaten until stiff. Continue folding in only until you can no longer see the whites separately. Pour 1/3 of the batter into each cake pan, smooth batter on top with spatula, and bake at 275 degrees for 45 minutes or until layers pull away from the sides of the forms slightly. Do not let the layers bake until they get too dry.

PARISIAN CREAM FROSTING-FILLING

2 cups whipping cream
6 tablespoons Dröste cocoa
1 cup sugar
pinch of salt

Mix ingredients in bowl and let stand at least 2 hours, or overnight, in refrigerator. Whip until stiff, but do not overbeat. Set bottom layer of cake on plate and cover with filling. Set second layer on top of first and spread filling on it. Do the same with the third layer, using a spatula to smooth the filling over top and sides.

PTAČKY ("BIRDS")

2 pounds beef, elk, or venison
1/4 pound onion, sliced
1/4 pound julienne bacon strips,
   uncooked
salt
butter for browning
1 to 2 tablespoons flour
Chablis wine (enough to make
   gravy of desired consistency)
4 tablespoons prepared yellow
   mustard (1 teaspoon per "bird")
3 or 4 large dill pickles
freshly ground pepper
1 cup sour cream
fresh or canned whole mushroom tops

Slice meat and pound it into pieces 1/2 inch thick and about 3 inches long. Sprinkle each piece with salt and pepper, and spread with mustard. On each piece of meat, place 2 strips of onion, 2 strips of dill pickle, and 2 julienne strips of uncooked bacon. Fold meat over along 2 edges to keep filling from falling out, and then roll up "bird" from 1 of the 2 unfolded ends. Tie with string or secure with toothpicks. Put butter in a cast-iron pot and sear "birds" on both sides until light brown. Cover the pot and reduce heat; cook until the gravy is golden brown. Continue to simmer for about 1 hour, adding boiling water as needed, until "birds" are well done. Thicken the gravy with sour cream, Chablis, and flour, and sprinkle with mushrooms. Serve with sweet-sour cabbage. Makes about 12 "birds."

"We always put nutmeg on vegetables and on ground meat . . . I was very surprised to learn they put it in cookies here."

DUTCH

"It was the worst trip the Holland-American Line ever made," says Magdalena Post van der Burg of her stormy December crossing of the Atlantic in 1956. "Water came streaming down the stairs till people were standing to their middles in it, and all the furniture came unbolted and went back and forth, from the crib in our stateroom to the piano in the salon." Undaunted by the rough voyage and the challenges of adjusting to life in a new country, however, Magdalena did not take long to prove that America is still the land of opportunity.

Only five months after they came to Boulder, Colorado, with their four children, Willem and Magdalena Post van der Burg were invited to a PTA potluck dinner at the children's school. "I didn't know what to take to the dinner; so my husband advised me to make Dutch-style pound cakes,"says Magdalena."Everyone loved the delicious, fine-grained cakes and said, 'Why don't you make them for sale and we will be your customers!' " Soon she and Willem, helped by the children, were turning out 60 pound cakes a week, working from early morning till late at night because their apartment-size oven held only two loaf pans. Clasina, then 13, used the children's wagon for door-to-door sales and deliveries, and sons Willem, Hans, and Gerard were soon part of the family business.

As cake sales expanded out over Colorado and Wyoming, the business moved to larger and larger quarters, and the Post van der Burgs set up long tables at which local customers could enjoy not only the famous cakes, but homemade soups, salads, and sandwiches. By 1968, Willem and Magdalena had opened Magdalena's Famous Holland Restaurant and Delicatessen, a full-fledged restaurant seating 150 and featuring authentic Dutch hot plates. A gift shop at the front of the restaurant offered almond, lemon, and vanilla pound cakes for sale, as well as imported toys, jewelry, porcelain, and foods, especially Holland chocolate. In 1973 the Post van der Burgs left the restaurant business to open a larger gift shop, also called Magdalena's, where the famous pound cake (the recipe must remain a secret even from readers of this cookbook) is once again being sold.

An outstanding favorite among the homemade soups, hearty sandwiches, and filling hot plates at Magdalena's restaurant was *hutspot,* Holland's famous national hot dish. A tasty blend of fresh Dutch country-style potatoes and separately cooked carrots and onions, *hutspot* goes back to 1574, when the Spaniards had besieged Leyden, a university city north of The Hague. Although there are bulb fields around Leyden now, until about a hundred years ago there was only sea between Haarlem and Leyden. Prince William of Orange and his men sailed overland to the rescue, breaking dikes at night and advancing in the morning, until on October 3 they reached the city and ended the siege. The starving citizens fell upon the supplies of carrots, onions, and potatoes brought by William's troops, cooking them on the spot. October 3 is still a national holiday, when Dutch around the world eat *hutspot,* and bread loaves and herring are distributed in Leyden. When served with stewed lean beef, as it was at Magdalena's, this dish is called *hutspot met klapstuk,* hot dish with beef.

Another favorite Dutch hot dish is *haché,* hashed meat. A stick-to-the-ribs mixture of stew meat and onions, it, like *hutspot,* is eaten in the winter in Holland. Magdalena, however, found that Americans demanded her hot plates year-round! In Holland *haché* is served over cooked, cubed potatoes, but since Magdalena's customers did not know what to do with it served that way, she served it with a slice of pumpernickel or rye bread. During Holland's cold, raw winters, soup is also an important part of the menu, and the most typically Dutch soup is *erwtensoep,* pea soup, a thick, steaming combination of peas, leeks, pigs' feet, celery, smoked sausage, and special spices.

Willem comments, ''Dutch eating is flavorful, but simpler than in America. Meat is always cooked in a dutch oven on top of the stove, never in the oven. At the restaurant all we cooked in the oven was just cakes and cookies. And when we have turkey at home, we even cook that on top of the stove. At home when we have guests, we will have potatoes, two or three vegetables, bread, relishes, and salad. But when we are 'together,' just us, we have vegetables and meat, and Magdalena fixes potatoes just for me, not for her.''

There is much more to Dutch cooking, of course, than the main dishes that made Magdalena's famous. *Poffertjes,* puffy little yeast fritters, are made and sold hot from the stove at special *krams* or little open-air tent-shops in such cities as Amsterdam and the Post van der Burgs' native Rotterdam. ''Each town has its own famous shop, with its own secret recipe,'' says Willem. ''And when we went back to visit not too long ago, the same people as before were running the one in Rotterdam. They have a huge stove, black from years of cooking, and on it a big flat iron plate with rows of shallow round depressions — six, twelve, or eighteen each way. The man skillfully whips down the rows putting a little batter in each hole with a huge spoon. Then they have to be turned with a fork when they are brown on top, and the man's hand goes down the rows like a machine. It is the same to pick them up when both sides are brown. Then they put butter and powdered sugar on them, and the people eat them while they are still hot.''

Another yeast-based recipe is that for *drie in de pan,* little pancakes cooked ''three in the pan'' and filled with currants and raisins. And on a cold winter evening nothing tastes better with hot pastries than *anijsmelk,* anise milk, a simple yet subtle blend of milk, sugar, anise, and cornstarch. In Holland, skaters buy anise milk at a *Koek en Zoopie,* Cook and Drink, a little unroofed hut built right on the ice, where the proprietor sells cookies, and fills the skaters' cups with anise milk from a pot kept on a small stove.

Pepernoten are small cakes especially popular on December 5, Saint Nicholas's Eve, the traditional time for exchanging presents in Holland. Unlike our Santa Claus, the Dutch Saint Nicholas arrives from Spain, dressed in sweeping red bishop's robes, and accompanied by a Moorish servant, *Zwarte Piet,* Black Peter. In Dutch homes, Saint Nicholas's coming signals the appearance of marzipan, spiced cookies and cakes, chocolates, and *baketletter,* a pastry initial filled with almond paste. One spice not found in Dutch cookies, according to Magdalena, is nutmeg: "We always put nutmeg on vegetables, and on ground meat too, in Holland, but not in cookies. I was very surprised to learn they put it in cookies here."

GROENE ERWTENSOEP (GREEN PEA SOUP)

1 1/2 pounds uncooked split
  peas (700 grams)
about 1 pound ham hock
2 leeks (or onions)
2 tablespoons chopped parsley
2 medium carrots, diced
3 quarts water (3 liters)

about 1 pound spareribs
1 cup chopped celery stalks
  and leaves
1 celery root, peeled and
  cut into 1/2-inch squares
salt, to taste

Let peas soak overnight in water. Bring to a boil next day in same water, with the leeks, celery root, and salt. Also put in the ham hock and spareribs and let them cook with the other ingredients. Let simmer about 4 hours, stirring frequently. When soup is done, put in the chopped parsley. Take out the meat and remove the meat from the bone. Cut meat into small pieces, and put into the soup. Serves 6 to 7.

ANIJSMELK (ANISE MILK)

4 cups (1 liter) milk,
  with 1/2 cup set aside
2 tablespoons aniseed (10 grams)
1 tablespoon cornstarch
  (8 grams) (optional)

3 to 4 tablespoons sugar
  (40 grams), or to taste

Tie aniseed in small pieces of cheesecloth with string or thread. Set aside 1/2 cup milk. Let aniseed brew or soak in the rest of the milk for about 1 hour in a warm place. Remove aniseed; dissolve sugar in milk. Bring milk and sugar to a full boil. Mix cornstarch with the 1/2 cup of cold milk and pour this mixture into the hot milk-and-sugar mixture, stirring constantly, for about 3 minutes. Serve hot (from a little Dutch ''milk kettle,'' if you have one). Serves 4.

HACHÉ (STEWED MEAT)

2 pounds stew meat,
  cut into 1-inch cubes

1/4 cup butter
1 teaspoon salt, or to taste

enough cornstarch for right consistency of gravy
water for cooking

5 pounds yellow onions, chopped
1 bay leaf
freshly ground pepper, to taste

Brown meat on all sides in butter in heavy pan. Put in just enough water to cover, but not too much, and simmer, covered, for about 4 hours. Remove meat and put in onions, along with salt, pepper, and bay leaf. Simmer in the gravy until done, about 45 minutes. Put the meat back in, and thicken the gravy with cornstarch. Add more salt and pepper, to taste. Serve over cooked, cut-up potatoes, or with a slice of bread. Serves 6 to 8.

POFFERTJES (YEAST PUFFS)

2 1/4 to 2 1/2 cups sifted flour (250 grams)
2 eggs
2 packages dry yeast (20 grams
  cake yeast)
pinch of salt
melted butter to brush on munk pan*
2/3 cup lukewarm milk (1 1/2 deciliters)
2/3 cup lukewarm water (1 1/2 deciliters)
powdered sugar

Sift flour into bowl. Make a well in the middle of the flour and break eggs into it, stirring eggs into flour. Mix lukewarm water and lukewarm milk together, and dissolve yeast in 1/2 cup of it. Stir yeast back into rest of water and milk, and add to flour mixture. Beat batter very fast with a spoon for 6 minutes. Cover and let rise 30 to 60 minutes. Grease holes in heated munk pan with melted butter. Pour 1 tablespoon of batter into each hole, so that hole is half full. When poffertjes look lightly browned on bottom but are still soft in the middle, turn with fork or knitting needle and let other side brown. The poffertjes close into hollow balls when done, and should be served hot with powdered sugar. Makes about 7 or 8 dozen.

---

*A munk pan is a heavy cast-iron frying pan 7 or 8 inches wide, with circular depressions in it. A/S Jøtul's 7-hole munk pan is distributed in many areas by Scandicrafts, 5447 Satsuma Avenue, North Hollywood, California 91601.

HUTSPOT (DUTCH NATIONAL HOT DISH)

6 medium potatoes, peeled *
5 medium carrots, scraped
   and cut up*
1 teaspoon salt, or to taste
1/2 cup water for cooking
   carrots and onions

1/8 teaspoon ground pepper,
   or to taste
3 medium onions, chopped *
1/4 cup butter, or to taste
salted water for cooking
   potatoes

Put carrots and onions on rack in bottom of pressure cooker, add 1/2 cup water, and sprinkle with salt. Cook 9 minutes at 15-pound pressure. Peel and halve potatoes and cook in salted water until done. Drain carrots and onions and save the juice. Drain and dry potatoes and mix butter into them, mashing well. Put carrots, onions, and pepper in with potatoes and mash well, adding enough juice from the onions and carrots, at the end, to give the *hutspot* a good consistency. Serve with thinly sliced roast beef, clear meat juice, and dark bread. Serves 6 to 8.

DRIE IN DE PAN (THREE IN THE PAN)

5/8 cup whole-wheat flour
   (100 grams)
1 egg
3/4 cup lukewarm milk (1 3/4 deciliter)
   (set aside 1/3 cup for dissolving yeast)
3/4 teaspoon salt (5 grams)
total of 4 1/4 ounces (120 grams)
   currants and raisins
1 7/8 to 2 cups white flour
2 packages dry yeast (200 grams cake yeast)
butter for frying pancakes

Sift both flours into bowl. Make a well in the middle. Put the egg in the well. Dissolve yeast in 1/3 cup lukewarm milk; put into well, along with part of the rest of the milk. Stir out from the

---

* Magdalena's original recipe, serving about 20, called for 11 pounds potatoes, 5 pounds onions, 3 pounds carrots, and 1 pound butter.

middle into the flour, mixing everything into a thick batter. Beat 6 minutes with wooden spoon. Put in the rest of the milk, along with the currants, raisins, and salt. Mix well and round up in greased bowl. Cover bowl and put into kettle of warm water, without letting water get into bowl, and put cover on kettle. Let rise 1 hour. Heat and butter a skillet or griddle. Scoop out enough batter to make three 3-inch pancakes and put on skillet or griddle. Brown on both sides. Serve hot with sugar. Serves 3 to 4.

"We came to Juarez from Durango
with four burros and a horse."

MEXICAN

In Carmen Razo's spacious modern kitchen, a skillet full of piping-hot bean filling is ready on the stove, white flour *tortillas* are kept warm in towels in a shallow bucket, and the final step in making *burritos* is at hand. "A lot of people like it better with *chorizo*," she says, slapping a generous spoonful of the tasty mixture onto a *tortilla*. "The kids go to the ball game and they come and say, 'Mrs. Razo, make me some *burritos*. I'll pay you, but make them like last time.' They are the most popular food. Some people like *burritos* with cooked potato, cut in real tiny pieces, and put in with the beans. You should see the flavor they give to those *burritos!*

"I used to do housework, and my ladies would tell me to cook for them. There was a dentist's family I used to cook for most every day, and their kids were crazy about *chiles rellenos*. I made some with burger, and some with plain cheese, to take the 'hot' out of the pepper. The boys used to say, 'We don't care what else you make, but don't forget the *chiles rellenos!*' And the little kid in the house behind us comes in the kitchen almost every day and says, 'Gran'ma, *'tillas?*' He slaps his hands together to show he wants one, and then he goes and gets one from the bucket and eats it with butter. No, it doesn't bother me; I'm so used to kids."

Carmen has brought up not only her own five children, but seven others so equally her own that no outsider can keep track of which are which. "When the kids were gone, I

was lonely,'' she says. Her husband Romaldo, forty years a
miner, put up a show of stern reluctance each time, warning
her she would have to keep them neatly dressed and well
attended to. Then, long before women's lib was ever heard
of, he shouldered extra chores to help her do it. ''He said,
'You take care of the kids, and I'll work in the kitchen,' ''
Carmen says. ''He used to get up at 4 A.M. to sweep and
put out the trash; he said he enjoyed doing it. He still makes
all our flour *tortillas*, just in his hands, the old way, not in a
press. And he still picks his own *chile* and keeps it frozen.''
The Razos' neat yard, with a small shrine, birdfeeders, and
flowers of every color and species, is also Romaldo's work,
and he still gardens for a few families.

Carmen's childhood years were sometimes hard, but
never dull: ''We traveled all around Mexico, with the kids
born in Jalisco, Monterey, and Durango. Sometimes we
were on top on the world, and sometimes working, and we
often slept in the desert. We came to Juarez from Durango
with four burros and a horse, and stayed about three years.
My daddy used to have a stand with ice cream, sodas, candy,
and fruits, or he would get watermelons and a chunk of ice
and put a little table in front of the ice. Then in 1918 the flu
came, and all the people got sick and went broke. My sister
and brother and I did not get it, but it took six months for
our parents and uncle to get better. So many died that there
were no funerals, just trucks carrying bodies to the big
graves.

''Then we came to the United States in 1919, when I was
still a child. My mother used to have a restaurant in New
Mexico, and you should have seen the people come on
Saturdays and Sundays — I used to wash dishes all day long!
She was a good cook; I don't think I cook like her, but I try.
She used coal stoves with ovens in them to make the bread,
and used to make *tortillas* in the morning for the whole day
because it would get so hot you couldn't stand it. And she'd
make a big bowl of *chili* for three or four days and keep it in
the ice box. We took that ice box everywhere we moved; she
loved it. This is her *molcajete* that I smash the *chiles* in, and

the stone for it is a *tejolote.* She had it when she was a young girl and it is just plain rock, not like they make nowadays. I'm going to give it to my oldest daughter.''

Holiday celebrations were a welcome break in this hard-working life. Carmen says, ''For Christmas my mother used to make lots of little cookies and candies, and we had *piñatas* to break with sticks. She made little packages of colored paper to put in the tree, along with the candles; the tree was the nicest thing we had all year. There were just small things in the packages, two pennies, or a barrette, but when Christmas Day came we would go crazy opening them. It was the little kids' day, and they were not supposed to do anything except run and play. After everybody walked the two miles home from 6 A.M. Mass, people brought food and drinks, and pretty soon they began to dance. My daddy had a wonderful phonograph and used to crank it.''

In Mexico, parties called the *Posadas,* the Inns, are held from December 16 to 24, in memory of Joseph's and Mary's weary search for shelter in Bethlehem. After a short religious service, the blindfolded children take turns trying to break the *piñata* with a stick. Suspended above the children by a rope, the *piñata* is a container covered with tissue paper to resemble a bird, animal, or other object with child-appeal. When it is broken, fruits, candies, and small gifts spill on the ground for the children.

January 6, *El Día de los Reyes,* the Day of the Kings, is also an occasion for parties, and for the serving of *Rosca de los Reyes,* Kings' Ring. This yeast bread, filled with fruit, is baked in a ring and studded with candied fruits and nuts. Hidden inside is a tiny china doll, or a lima bean, and whoever finds it must then give another party the following February 2, Candlemas Day.

''Mexicans don't celebrate Easter like here,'' observes Carmen. ''It is more Christmas and New Year's. We always had fried sweets called *buñuelos* for New Year's, and the kids could stay up till after twelve, and jump and play. But after the New Year was born, everybody had to go to sleep except the grown-ups. Our father would take us outside and

say, 'Look, there's a little cloud; that is the New Year that
has been born.' After he showed us the sign in the sky and
we saw it was born, we believed him and went to bed.''

As famous as *buñuelos* is *pan de muerto*, bread of the
dead, traditional for All Souls' Day, November 2. Decorated
with dough teardrops and bones which form a cross, this
round coffee cake is taken along when the family visits its
graves in the cemetery. However, as Carmen says, ''The
Spanish people care more for desserts than the Mexican
people do. We used to eat a fresh apple or orange, never pies
and cake like these days.''

Among the Aztecs, chocolate was forbidden to women,
and only men of high rank were allowed to drink it.
Chocolatl, bitter water, was so highly prized by the Aztecs
that the seeds or beans from which it was brewed came to be
used as money. The Spanish conquerors of Mexico added
sugar and spices to this royal beverage, but continued the
custom of beating chocolate with a *molinillo* until it is
frothy. The Mexican chocolate available in many stores is
mixed with ground almonds, cinnamon, and cloves, plus
egg to make it foamier, but chocolate worthy of the Emperor
Montezuma can also be made with unsweetened chocolate,
sugar, ground cinnamon, and a blender.

Mexican food is thought of as ''hot,'' but Carmen is a
conservative: ''Too much garlic does not taste good,'' she
says with emphasis. And as to *chile* sauce: ''When my
daughter makes it, she uses a big bunch of *chiles,* so your
mouth is on fire. I don't like it that strong! Some people
make it with more tomato than *chile*, some use a lot of *chile*
and some tomato, and some even make plain *chile,* and that
is real hot. I don't see how you can eat that!''

ABOUT *CHILES*

Before using fresh *chiles*, rinse them in cold water, blister their skins, and peel them. Blister *chiles* on a flat metal plate fitted over burner, or in lard in a skillet, turning them frequently, until they are lightly browned but not limp (about 15 minutes total time). Put roasted *chiles* into plastic bag, closing it when all are done. After 10 minutes, peel *chiles*. (Or wrap *chiles* in damp cloth for 30 minutes after roasting, and then peel.) Peeled *chiles* can be refrigerated or frozen in clear plastic wrap.

If you used canned *chiles*, choose plain *chiles*, not *chiles* in sauces. Drain them, rinse them, and remove seeds. *Chiles* are milder when seeds are removed, and even milder when soaked several hours in slightly salty cold water.

Keep hands away from face and eyes while handling *chiles*, and always wash hands with soap and water afterward. Never rinse *chiles* in warm water, because it releases their oils into the air. Even a little *chile* in the eyes is very painful.

Ordinary green bell peppers may be substituted for green California *chiles*, but do not expect the same flavor.

CHILES RELLENOS (STUFFED *CHILES*)

5 long yellow *chiles*
  (or 5 California green *chiles*,
  or 5 green bell peppers)
1/2 pound longhorn cheese,
  coarsely shredded (less if you
  use meat and potatoes)
3 eggs, separated

flour
1/2 pound (or less) ground
  beef, browned (optional)
bacon grease or cooking oil
  for frying
1 large potato, cooked and
  finely diced (optional)

Slit roasted, peeled *chiles* lengthwise on one side almost to top. Remove seeds but leave stem on as a handle. Stuff *chiles* with shredded cheese, or with browned ground beef, alone or mixed with cheese; or stuff with diced, cooked potato mixed with cheese and/or meat. Use toothpicks to keep *chiles* closed. These stuffed *chiles* may be frozen. Beat 3 egg whites until fluffy, and add to 3 beaten yolks. Roll *chiles* in flour, then dip them in the egg batter (if stem "handle" has come off, take out of batter with two forks). Remove *chiles* from batter and put in skillet with about 1 inch of grease or oil which is medium hot. (If grease is too hot, egg batter will burn.) When *chiles* are golden brown on one side, turn with fork or spatula and fry other side golden brown. Drain *chiles* on paper towels and place on cookie sheet in warm oven until ready to serve. Makes 5 *chiles rellenos.*

CHILE VERDE (GREEN *CHILE* WITH PORK)

1 1/2 pounds pork roast
16-ounce can tomatoes
1 clove garlic, crushed
hot bacon grease (about
  1 to 2 tablespoons)
water

4 green California *chiles,*
  roasted and peeled
1 small onion, diced
2 tablespoons flour

Cut pork into 1-inch cubes and brown on all sides in hot grease. Remove meat from grease and boil until tender in enough water to cover. Put onion and flour into hot grease, add 2 cups of stock obtained from boiling pork cubes, and make a gravy. In a separate pan or bowl, smash roasted and peeled *chiles,* add tomatoes and crushed garlic and smash them, and mix all three thoroughly. Add this mixture to the gravy, then add the cooked pork cubes, and simmer 30 minutes. Serves 3 to 4. *Chile verde* is good on rice, and it may also be used as topping for *burritos.*

FRIJOLES REFRITOS (REFRIED BEANS)

3 cups pinto beans, uncooked
salt, to taste

4 cups water
3 tablespoons bacon grease

Clean and wash beans (but do not soak) and cook until tender (about 3 hours) in 4 cups water. If water is added during cooking, it must be boiling hot, or the beans will turn black. In a separate pan, heat 3 tablespoons bacon grease, add cooked beans without juice, and smash. Add salt to taste, mix all ingredients well, adding enough bean juice to make the *refritos* creamy, and cook until the beans are thickened, stirring frequently. As a side dish, serves 6.

SPANISH RICE

1 cup white rice, uncooked   8-ounce can tomato sauce
1/2 clove garlic, crushed   1 small piece of onion, diced
water (about 3 cups)   bacon grease (about 3 tablespoons)

Fry uncooked rice in grease until quite brown. Remove from heat and drain off the grease. Mix onion and garlic into the rice. Add tomato sauce and water and let simmer, covered, 25 to 30 minutes, or until rice is tender and fluffy. Serves 4 to 6.

MENUDO (TRIPE SOUP)

2 pounds honeycomb tripe   2 pig's feet cut in 4 pieces
about 6 tablespoons chili   (optional)
   powder (depending on how dark 1 small onion, cut in half
   or light a red color you want) 1-inch piece of lemon peel
2 tablespoons flour   1 to 2 teaspoons salt,
16-ounce can white hominy   or to taste
about 2 quarts water   1 cup diced green onions
a pinch of oregano

Wash tripe and cut into 1-inch cubes. Put tripe, onion, and lemon peel in kettle of water and cook until tripe is tender, about 1 1/2 hours (pinch a piece to see if it is tender but not soft). Make a paste or gravy as follows: brown 2 tablespoons flour in a pan without fat and let cool. Mix browned flour with the chili powder and make a paste by adding cold water, a spoonful at a time. Mix paste until smooth and creamy. Add paste and hominy to *menudo* and let simmer 10 minutes. Add salt and oregano. Sprinkle with diced green onions and/or diced onion, and oregano. Serves 5 to 6.

BURRITOS (LITTLE BURROS)

12 white flour *tortillas* (7-inch-diameter, sold frozen throughout
   the West, and available canned in specialty stores)
3/4 pound *chorizo* sausages or sausage mix (or substitute

smoked, spiced pork sausage which has been skinned and chopped up, or pep up regular pork sausage with 1 teaspoon *chile* powder (*not* chili powder), 1 teaspoon oregano, and 1/4 teaspoon liquid hot-pepper seasoning)
3 green California *chiles*
2 cups (1 pound) pinto beans, uncooked
1/4 pound longhorn cheese, shredded

Cook beans until tender, as in *frijoles refritos* recipe. Remove casings from *chorizo* and fry contents over low heat. Roast and peel *chiles* and smash until smooth. Smash cooked beans until very smooth. Combine *chorizo, chiles,* and beans; cook 10 to 15 minutes over low heat. Add shredded longhorn cheese. When cheese has melted and is mixed well, spread mixture onto *tortillas* and roll them up. Serve at once, or keep warm in oven. Makes 12 *burritos.*

CHOCOLATE

1 cake of Mexican chocolate, about 2 ounces (or 2 ounces un-
    sweetened chocolate, melted and mixed with 2 tablespoons
    sugar, 1 teaspoon cinnamon, and 1/8 teaspoon salt)
4 cups milk (heated)

Put Mexican chocolate (or the substitute mixture) into hot milk, and keep over low heat until chocolate melts, stirring frequently. Do not let it come to a boil. Twirl *molinillo* (a carved wooden beater) between hands until its knobbed end and loose wooden rings make the chocolate foam, or do this in blender. Then let chocolate come to a boil (the foam will disappear) and serve hot. More sugar may be added if desired. Makes 4 cups.

"Russians don't make many salads,
  but they are good on soups and
  on combined foods, like casseroles"

RUSSIAN

"In Russia the dining room is the center of the house, and all the activities are there," says Vera Karpoff, briskly settling herself before the *samovar* on her dining room table, and passing a plate of meat-filled *pirozhki* fresh from the oven. The original *samovars,* self-boilers, were ornate urns filled with water and heated by a charcoal fire in a central vertical tube, but modern ones are heated electrically.

Vera pours concentrated tea into each cup from the china teapot, and then dilutes it with hot water from the samovar before passing it. "This shallow glass bowl is called a *poloskatel 'nitsa,* from the verb 'to rinse,' " she explains. "I use this slotted spoon to take tea leaves out of the cups and empty them into the bowl, and then I rest the spoon across the bowl. In old Russia, men did not drink from a regular teacup, but from a glass which fitted into an engraved silver holder with a handle. But women always drank from a dainty cup."

Konstantin, her husband, adds, "In every railway station you could buy *pirozhki* and hot boiling water for tea, to fix right in your compartment. But the best *pirozhki* are Tartar *pirozhki,* which are filled with raw meat, and then fried instead of baked. Vera usually serves *pirozhki* with *vinegret* for Russians, but with some other salad for Americans." It is only natural that Konstantin prefers Tartar *pirozhki,* since he grew up in Tashkent, in the Central Asian steppes of Russia. There, near the borders of China, Afghanistan, and Iran, the food savors of Persia, and lamb reigns supreme — in dumplings; *shashlik; shish kebab;* and *plov,* pilaff.

Vera grew up in Vladivostok because her father was a civil engineer working on a project there, but he was originally from the Ural region, and her mother came from Kiev, in the Ukraine. *Vostok* is the Russian word for ''east,'' and Vladivostok, the eastern terminus of the 4000-mile Trans-Siberian Railroad, lies on the Sea of Japan, near the border between Korea and Manchuria.

''In January in Vladivostok it was minus 40 degrees,'' says Vera, recalling the way people there celebrated the Russian Twelfth Night. ''On Epiphany they would cut a chunk of ice out of the bay in the form of a cross, and set it up. Then there was a procession from the cathedral with ikons and banners, the orchestras marching, and the choirs singing with their noses frozen. There was a service, and a blessing of the water in the hole left in the ice by the cross. Some who felt specially moved to do it would jump naked into that hole and then out again and into fur coats, to be cleansed of their sins. And if they believed in it, it probably helped them!

''I think traditions are wonderful,'' Vera says with conviction. ''They look unnecessary, but no, you can't do everything by machines. They do decorate our sometimes very gray lives; they give a little beauty, and help us endure many things, too.''

During the early years of their marriage, the Karpoffs lived in Harbin, Manchuria, where Konstantin earned an engineering degree from the Chinese Institute of Technology and Vera worked long hours as a seamstress. ''I would buy a pound of meat,'' says Vera, ''and he would make a dinner by making soup, skimming the fat, and frying the potatoes. On weekends I cooked, and often made *pel'meni*. These are little pieces of dough filled with ground beef, salt, pepper, and onion, like *ravioli*. They were good because people could freeze them outside for the whole winter, and boil them quickly when they wanted to eat them.''

When the Karpoffs came to California in the late twenties, Konstantin studied engineering at Berkeley. Once he was working as an engineer, he and Vera became the parents of a son, Konstantin Konstantinovich, and Vera, like Russian mothers the world around, continued to cook the old-country foods.

"Russians don't make many salads," says Vera, "but they are good on soups, and on combined foods, like casseroles. Most Russian cookery requires less meat, but more time to prepare. The spices are not unusual, though dill is used a lot, and the vegetables are not at all fancy. Russians are very fond of *zakuski* of all kinds — herring, ham, boiled salad, beets, sauerkraut, pickles, potatoes, caviar."

Zakuski, small bites, are appetizers brought from Scandinavia by the Rurik dynasty (the French renamed them *hors d'oeuvres* when they adopted them in the 1800s). Because of stormy weather and bad roads, Russian guests might arrive at any hour, and a table laden with vodka and *zakuski* allowed hostesses to welcome cold, hungry guests with substantial food whether or not the main courses were ready.

Instead of celebrating birthdays, Russians celebrate the name day, or *imeniny.* Vera says, "All your friends come; so you have a *pirog.* This is like *pirozhki,* except it is on a cookie sheet. It's a sheet cake, but with a different texture. It can be with meat, with cabbage and eggs, or with jam or a sweet, and is very Russian. But the *pirozhki* are easier; there is no fork, and no cutting."

When the first star can be seen on Christmas Eve, it is a Russian custom to break the Advent fast with *kutia,* an ancient Slavonian dish which is also eaten by mourners at Orthodox funerals. *Kutia* is made by mixing a tablespoon of honey and a half cup of sugar with one cup of hot, drained, boiled rice, then sprinkling a half cup of raisins over it. In some areas of Russia, walnuts are added; in other, *kutia* is made with cooked whole wheat instead of rice, with poppy seeds mixed in.

The Russian Lent is a grim one, banning not only meat, but milk and eggs as well. To fortify themselves for its rigors, the Russians celebrate the week before as *maslenitsa,* butter week, which is given over to masks and costumes, parties, and above all, *bliny.* These paper-thin pancakes, once a pagan symbol of the sun's return after the long winter darkness, are traditionally eaten with butter and sour cream, and are also served with fish and caviar, or even stuffed with chopped mushrooms and onions.

The 40 days of fasting past, Easter, the religious and culinary climax of the Russian year, brings an explosion of foods long untasted — eggs with shells decorated in intricate geometrical patterns, hams and other meats, and endless varieties of *zakuski*. Tall, cylindrical loaves of *kulich* wrapped in white napkins are blessed at the church, along with the dyed eggs. When the midnight bells ring out, the worshippers carry their lighted candles around the church three times, greeting one another with "*Khristos voskres!*" — "Christ is risen!"

The feasting begins right after church, and the twin centers of attention at the table are the rich, sweet bread called *kulich,* and the *paskha,* a flat-topped pyramid of cream cheese. "Easter is the holiday of holidays," Vera says. "Everyone has open house, and the food has been done ahead of time. *Kulich* can be baked two weeks before, but my mother said in Kiev they always did it on the Thursday before. It is in the form of a mountain, for Calvary. She said they always prepared the eggs on Thursday too, but there were never any faces on the eggs. I was surprised at some American designs with people on them; they seemed almost sacrilegious!"

Vera makes her *paskha* in a special wooden form Konstantin made for her, 5¾ inches high, with each of the four sides 5¾ inches wide at the bottom of the pyramid, but a clay flowerpot with a hole in the bottom may be used instead: "Konstantin decorates our *paskha* with chocolate icing at the corners, and with flowers, a cross, and *XB,* the Russian initials for *Khristos voskres.*"

Summing up what cooking means to her, Vera says, "I started to cook because I like to eat. I like to taste and I like to cook; so I am experimenting continually. I am really crazy about cooking; I have scrapbooks and everything. And I like to give the recipes and let other people be enjoying them; I don't want to keep them back."

VARENIKI (DESSERT DUMPLINGS) WITH CHERRIES

FILLING
3 cups pitted cherries, uncooked   2 tablespoons flour
1/2 cup sugar
Mix these 3 ingredients to make the filling.

DOUGH
1/2 cup water   3 eggs
4 to 5 cups sifted flour   1 teaspoon salt
  (depending on egg size)

COOKING AND SERVING
1/4 cup melted butter (about)   sour cream (optional)
kettle of salted water (about   sugar (optional)
  1 quart water and 1 teaspoon salt)

Put flour into large mixing bowl, scoop out a deep hollow in the flour, and put eggs, salt, and water into hollow. Slowly mix flour into other ingredients and knead into very stiff dough. If it crumbles, add a little more water. Let dough stand 15 minutes to 1 hour. Make 2 ''logs'' from the dough, about 2 inches in diameter. Slice ''logs'' into circles about 1/2 inch thick, and, with floured rolling pin on floured board, roll each circle until about 1/4 inch thick. Put filling on one half of each circle and fold the other half over to cover the filling, forming a filled half-circle. Pinch edges together to seal. Drop *vareniki* into kettle of boiling, salted water and let simmer uncovered 8 to 10 minutes, or until they come to the surface. Remove, drain, and put on shallow platter. Pour melted butter over *vareniki.* Serve hot. Top with sour cream and sugar if desired. Makes about 3 dozen.

BLINY (RUSSIAN PANCAKES)

3 eggs, separated
1/4 cup warm water
1 package dry yeast*
2 cups warm water
2 1/2 cups sifted flour
2 cups scalded milk
1 pint sour cream

1 tablespoon sugar
1 teaspoon salt
1/4 cup butter, melted
additional melted butter for
  topping bliny
16 ounces caviar or herring
  (optional)

Dissolve yeast in 1/4 cup warm water. Mix egg yolks with sugar, salt, and melted butter, and add to dissolved yeast. Stir the rest of the water into the mixture and add the flour gradually. Beat egg whites until stiff and add to mixture, folding them in carefully. Let rise until doubled in bulk (about 2 hours). Just before making bliny, scald the milk and pour it over the mixture at once. Mix well, as quickly as possible. Let rise 15 to 30 minutes. Lightly brush a 6-inch cast-iron frying pan with melted butter (or use an electric pancake griddle). Over high heat, ladle in about 1/2 cup batter to form one blin 3 to 4 inches wide (or make 6 bliny at a time on electric griddle). When top side of blin is almost done, turn it over and cook a few more minutes. Keep cooked bliny in warm oven until all are cooked. Serve topped with sour cream, melted butter, and caviar or herring. Many people like bliny with syrup. Serves 4 to 8.

PIROZHKI (LITTLE MEAT-FILLED PASTRIES)

FILLING (make first and let cool while you prepare dough)
1 large onion, chopped
1 pound ground beef
1/2 cup water

1 tablespoon fat or shortening
1 tablespoon flour

Sauté onion in fat until pink, but not brown. Add ground beef, stirring with fork to prevent formation of chunks. Cook only until no red is visible in the meat. Sprinkle with 1 tablespoon of flour, mix well, and add 1/2 cup water, mixing all ingredients thoroughly. Cool. Use to fill pirozhki dough.

---

* Vera uses 1 package at a 5,200-foot altitude; 1 1/2 packages should be used at sea level.

DOUGH

2 cups scalded milk, cooled
    to lukewarm
1/3 cup sugar
6 tablespoons butter

6 cups sifted flour (about)
1 package dry yeast *
1 teaspoon salt
2 eggs, slightly beaten

Add sugar and salt to milk, sprinkle with yeast, and mix well. Add melted butter and the eggs, and mix in. Gradually add flour, mixing and kneading about 5 minutes on floured board, as for bread dough. Form into a ball, grease lightly, cover with a towel, and let rise in warm, draft-free place about 2 hours, until doubled. Punch dough down and let rise again for about 30 to 60 minutes, or until dough is puffy. Take pieces of dough (of the size for dinner rolls) and flatten; with a floured rolling pin on a floured board, roll each piece into an oval about 3 inches long and about 1/4 inch thick. Put 1 tablespoon of filling along the center of the oval; close and seal edges of dough over filling. With the sealed sides down, place *pirozhki* on lightly greased, floured cookie sheet and bake in 375 degree oven about 20 minutes, or until nice and brown. Makes about 25 *pirozhki*.

PASKHA (EASTER DESSERT)

2 pounds pot cheese (*very* dry cottage cheese, *not* ordinary
    creamed kind; if necessary, drain moisture by setting cheese in
    colander, covering with thin cloth, and weighting it)
8 ounces cream cheese
1 1/2 cups unsalted butter, softened
1 pint whipping cream
1 teaspoon each: vanilla extract,
    ground nutmeg, cinnamon, and cloves
1/2 cup each: candied fruits,
    raisins, and chopped almonds
8 hard-boiled egg yolks
1 3/4 cups sugar

Alternately force cottage cheese, egg yolks, butter, and cream cheese through a meat grinder, 3 times. Cream together well. (Some people simply force cottage cheese and egg yolks through a sieve.) Whip cream; add it and rest of ingredients to mixture. Russians use a wooden mold shaped like an inverted pyramid for *paskha.* The mold is about 7 inches high, with inside width 3 inches on the bottom and 6 1/2 inches on the top. Possible substitutes for the pyramid-shaped wooden form are two unglazed clay 6-inch flowerpots (hole in the bottom of pot) or a 2-pound cottage-cheese carton with a hole cut in the bottom. The mold must have a hole so that excess liquid can escape, or else the *paskha* will be soggy. Line the mold with dampened cheesecloth, smoothing out wrinkles and poking cloth into corners, and let about 2 inches of cloth hang over the sides. Put the mixture into the mold, fold the extra cloth over the top, and put a weight on top of the cloth. Keep in refrigerator 1 hour, with something on the shelf below it to catch the liquid. Remove the weight and leave *paskha* in refrigerator overnight. To serve, unwrap cloth at top, put a plate over the top of the mold, and turn both over. Gently peel the cloth from the *paskha.* Decorate with additional almonds and candied fruits, or even artificial or candy flowers. Slice horizontally and serve alone, or spread *paskha* on slices of pound cake or *kulich. Paskha* will keep in the refrigerator for about a week after it is unmolded.

SOLYANKA (SAUERKRAUT CASSEROLE)

1-pound-11-ounce can of sauerkraut, rinsed in hot water and
   squeezed dry

2 strips of bacon, uncooked	1 large onion, chopped
1 medium carrot, shredded	1 apple, shredded
1 teaspoon salt	1/4 cup sugar
1/2 teaspoon caraway seeds	1 pound cooked ham, cubed
1/4 cup cooking oil	(optional)
(or liquid fat from ham)	1/4 cup water
1 teaspoon ground pepper	

Fry onion in oil until pink. Add sauerkraut, shredded carrot and apple, salt, sugar, caraway seeds, ground pepper, and water. Mix, put in large casserole, and lay strips of bacon on top. Bake at 350 degrees about 1 1/2 hours, and serve with pork or other meat. Or, 15 minutes before *solyanka* is done, add cooked ham to it. Serves 6 to 8.

MORKOV' (CARROTS)

1 large onion, chopped
4 or 5 medium carrots,
  coarsely shredded
4 or 5 medium parsnips,
  coarsely shredded
1 tablespoon sugar

1/4 cup cooking oil
1 large green pepper, chopped
8-ounce can tomato sauce
salt and pepper, to taste

Sauté onion in oil until pink. Add other ingredients and cook over low heat until vegetables are tender, stirring frequently. Serves 4 to 6.

LENTEN BORSHCH (LENTEN CABBAGE SOUP)

1/4 cup vegetable oil
1 heaping tablespoon flour
8-ounce can tomato sauce
2 large beets, cubed
1 tablespoon salt
peppercorns
1 large onion, chopped

1 bay leaf
2 quarts water
2 large carrots, cubed
1 1/2 pounds chopped raw
  cabbage
1 green pepper, chopped
(optional)

Sauté onion in oil. Add flour, and mix. Add water and mix well. Then add other ingredients and simmer over low heat for about 1 hour. Taste borshch to see if it needs more spices, or perhaps a little sugar. (If not interested in avoiding dairy products, serve accompanied by sour cream which each person can spoon into his soup.) Serves 6 to 8.